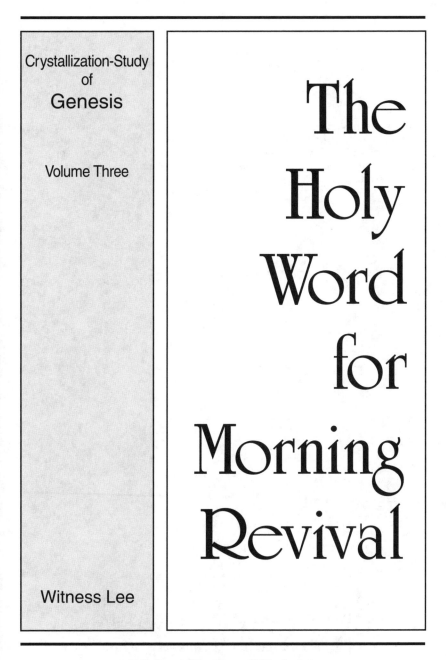

Crystallization-Study
of
Genesis

Volume Three

The
Holy
Word
for
Morning
Revival

Witness Lee

Living Stream Ministry
Anaheim, CA • www.lsm.org

First Edition, January 2014.

ISBN 978-0-7363-6827-8

Published by

Living Stream Ministry
2431 W. La Palma Ave., Anaheim, CA 92801 U.S.A.
P. O. Box 2121, Anaheim, CA 92814 U.S.A.

Printed in the United States of America

14 15 16 17 / 5 4 3 2 1

2013 Winter Training

CRYSTALLIZATION-STUDY OF GENESIS

Contents

Preface

1. This book is intended as an aid to believers in developing a daily time of morning revival with the Lord in His word. At the same time, it provides a limited review of the winter training held December 23-28, 2013, in Anaheim, California, on the continuation of the "Crystallization-study of Genesis." Through intimate contact with the Lord in His word, the believers can be constituted with life and truth and thereby equipped to prophesy in the meetings of the church unto the building up of the Body of Christ.

2. The book is divided into weeks. One training message is covered per week. Each week presents first the message outline, followed by six daily portions, a hymn, and then some space for writing. The training outline has been divided into days, corresponding to the six daily portions. Each daily portion covers certain points and begins with a section entitled "Morning Nourishment." This section contains selected verses and a short reading that can provide rich spiritual nourishment through intimate fellowship with the Lord. The "Morning Nourishment" is followed by a section entitled "Today's Reading," a longer portion of ministry related to the day's main points. Each day's portion concludes with a short list of references for further reading and some space for the saints to make notes concerning their spiritual inspiration, enlightenment, and enjoyment to serve as a reminder of what they have received of the Lord that day.

3. The space provided at the end of each week is for composing a short prophecy. This prophecy can be composed by considering all of our daily notes, the "harvest" of our inspirations during the week, and preparing a main point with some sub-points to be spoken in the church meetings for the organic building up of the Body of Christ.

4. Following the last week in this volume, we have provided reading schedules for both the Old and New Testaments in the Recovery Version with footnotes. These schedules are arranged so that one can read through both the Old and

New Testaments of the Recovery Version with footnotes in two years.

5. As a practical aid to the saints' feeding on the Word throughout the day, we have provided verse cards at the end of the volume, which correspond to each day's Scripture reading. These may be cut out and carried along as a source of spiritual enlightenment and nourishment in the saints' daily lives.

6. The content of this book is taken primarily from *Crystallization-study Outlines: Genesis (2)*, the text and footnotes of the Recovery Version of the Bible, selections from the writings of Witness Lee and Watchman Nee, and *Hymns*, all of which are published by Living Stream Ministry.

7. *Crystallization-study Outlines: Genesis (2)* was compiled by Living Stream Ministry from the writings of Witness Lee and Watchman Nee. The outlines, footnotes, and cross-references in the Recovery Version of the Bible are by Witness Lee. Unless otherwise noted, the references cited in this publication are by Witness Lee.

8. For the sake of space, references to *The Collected Works of Watchman Nee* and *The Collected Works of Witness Lee* are abbreviated to *CWWN* and *CWWL*, respectively.

Winter Training
(December 23-28, 2013)

CRYSTALLIZATION-STUDY
OF GENESIS

Banners:

We need to know and experience
the God of Abraham, the God of Isaac,
and the God of Jacob
to become the Israel of God,
the church in the Triune God.

If we would walk in the steps
of Abraham's faith,
we must be those who live the life
of the altar and the tent,
taking Christ as our life
and the church as our living
to live a life of being transfused by God,
consecrating our all to God,
and taking His presence as our road map.

The God of Abraham
is the God of speaking in His appearing, with
calling, in a vision,
and in the human friendship,
to unveil to His intimate friend on the earth
what He aspired for him to be
and what He wanted him to do
according to His heart's desire
for the accomplishment of the eternal
economy for the Divine Trinity.

After we offer to God
what we have received of Him
and what He has wrought into us,
He will return it to us in resurrection,
and we will believe in and experience God
as the God of resurrection
for the fulfillment of His purpose.

Knowing and Experiencing
the God of Abraham, the God of Isaac,
and the God of Jacob
to Become the Israel of God

Scripture Reading: Gen. 28:13; 33:20; Exo. 3:6, 14-15; Acts 3:13; Gal. 6:16; 1 Thes. 1:1

Day 1

I. **Our God is the God of three particular persons—Abraham, Isaac, and Jacob; this implies that He is the Triune God (Exo. 3:15; Matt. 28:19; 2 Cor. 13:14):**

A. Abraham, Isaac, and Jacob are the foundations of the nation of Israel; without them there would not be the nation of Israel (Exo. 3:15-16):

1. God's people became His people through the experiences of Abraham, Isaac, and Jacob; their experiences culminated in Israel, the people of God.

2. We all need to have the elements of Abraham, Isaac, and Jacob; without these elements we cannot be the people of God, the Israel of God.

B. In the book of Genesis the records of Abraham, Isaac, and Jacob overlap; Genesis does not portray them as three separate individuals but as constituents of one corporate person:

1. The experience of Abraham signifies the experience of God the Father, the unique source, in His calling man, justifying man, and equipping man to live by faith and to live in fellowship with Him (12:1; 15:6; chs. 17—18; 19:29; 21:1-13; 22:1-18).

2. The experience of Isaac signifies the experience of God the Son in His redeeming man and His blessing man with the inheritance of all His riches, with a life of the enjoyment of His abundance, and with a life in peace (vv. 1-14; 25:5; 26:3-4, 12-33).

3. The experience of Jacob (with Joseph) signifies the experience of God the Father in
His loving man and choosing man (Mal. 1:2;
Rom. 9:10-13) and of God the Spirit in His
causing all things to work together for the
good of those who love Him, in His trans-
forming man, and in His making man mature in the divine life so that man may be able
to bless all the people, rule over all the earth,
and satisfy all the people with God the Son
as the life supply (Gen. 27:41; 28:1—35:12;
chs. 37; 39—49; Rom. 8:28-29).

Day 2 II. **We need to know and experience the God of
Abraham, the God of Isaac, and the God of
Jacob:**

A. Abraham believed in God as the unique source,
as the One who "calls the things not being as
being" (4:17):

1. God's goal must be achieved according to
God's time and through God's power (Gen.
17:17, 19, 21).

2. God did a special work on Abraham in order
to show him what it means for God to be the
Father (Eph. 4:6):

a. To know God as the Father is to know
that He is the source, the unique Initiator, and that everything originates from
Him (Matt. 15:13).

b. We all need to know that God is the
Father and that everything proceeds
from Him (Rom. 11:36; 1 Cor. 8:6; Eph.
3:14-16).

B. In Isaac, the best figure of the Son, we see that
everything comes from the Father (Gen. 24:36;
25:5):

1. According to the picture in Genesis 22, Isaac
typifies Christ in a detailed way.

Day 3 2. The principle of Isaac is the principle of
receiving (25:5; 1 Cor. 4:7):

a. The significance of God the Son is that everything is received and that nothing is initiated by Him (John 16:15; 17:10; 5:19, 30).

b. In Isaac we see that everything comes from the Father and that our place is to receive (Gen. 26:12-13; Rom. 11:36; 1 Cor. 4:7):

(1) Isaac's relationship with Abraham was one of receiving; to know the God of Isaac is to know God as the Supplier (Gen. 24:36).

(2) God is the Father, and everything proceeds from Him; we are sons, and everything we have is from Him (1 Cor. 8:6; 11:12b).

C. Jacob speaks to us of the Holy Spirit; his experiences represent the work of the Holy Spirit, and his history is a type of the discipline of the Holy Spirit:

1. Jacob's life is a life that represents God's dealings, and the God of Jacob is the God of dealings (Gen. 31:38-41):

a. The title *the God of Jacob* implies how the Holy Spirit disciplined Jacob, dealt with his natural life, constituted Christ into him, and bore the fruit of the Spirit in him (Gal. 5:22-23; Heb. 12:11).

b. If we would know the God of Jacob, we need to allow the Spirit to perform His work in us, dealing with our natural life and constituting Christ into us.

Day 4

2. Jacob's history is a picture of the discipline of the Holy Spirit (Gen. 47:9; 48:15-16a; Heb. 12:9-11):

a. The discipline of the Holy Spirit refers to what the Holy Spirit is doing in our outward environment—to His arranging of all people, things, and happenings—

through which we are being disciplined (Rom. 8:28).

b. Through the discipline of the Holy Spirit, God completely tears down the element of the old creation in us so that the element of the new creation may be built up in us.

3. God deals with our natural life through the discipline of the Holy Spirit so that Christ may be wrought into us, constituted into us, and formed in us for the corporate expression of the Triune God (Gal. 4:19; Eph. 3:16-21).

D. The God of Abraham, the God of Isaac, and the God of Jacob is Jehovah, Elohim—the self-existing and ever-existing Triune God, the eternal great I Am (Exo. 3:6, 14; Rev. 1:4).

E. The God of Abraham, the God of Isaac, and the God of Jacob is the God of resurrection (Exo. 3:6, 15; Matt. 22:23-33; Acts 3:13).

F. The God of Abraham, the God of Isaac, and the God of Jacob is the God of the tabernacle; Abraham, Isaac, and Jacob each lived in a tent; while they were living in tents, they were eagerly waiting for the eternal tabernacle of God, the city of New Jerusalem (Exo. 40:34-35; Gen. 12:8; 13:18; 26:17, 25; 33:18; 35:21; Heb. 11:9-10; Rev. 21:2-3).

G. The God of Abraham is the God of justification (Gen. 15:6; Rom. 4:2-3), the God of Isaac is the God of grace (2 Cor. 13:14), and the God of Jacob is the God of transformation through divine discipline (3:18; Heb. 12:5-11); eventually, the God of Jacob became the God of Israel (Gen. 33:20; Exo. 5:1), the God of the transformed Jacob.

Day 5 III. **The issue of experiencing the God of Abraham, the God of Isaac, and the God of Jacob is the Israel of God, the church in the Triune God (Gen. 35:10; 33:20; Gal. 6:16; 1 Thes. 1:1; Matt. 28:19):**

A. The Israel of God is the real Israel (Rom. 9:6b; 2:28-29; Phil. 3:3), including all the Gentile and Jewish believers in Christ, who are the true sons of Abraham, who are the household of the faith, and who are those in the new creation (Gal. 3:7, 29; 6:10, 15-16):

1. The real Israel, the spiritual Israel, is the church (v. 16; Matt. 16:18).

2. In God's New Testament economy we have been made both the sons of God and the Israel of God; our destiny is to be sons of God expressing God and also kings reigning in the kingdom of God (Gal. 3:26; 6:10, 16; Rev. 5:10; 21:7; 22:5b; 12:5a).

3. As the Israel of God, we represent God, exercise His authority, and carry out His administration on earth for the fulfillment of His purpose (Gen. 1:26, 28; Luke 10:19; Rev. 12:5, 7-11).

Day 6

B. The Israel of God is the church in the Triune God (1 Thes. 1:1; Matt. 28:19):

1. When Paul speaks of the church in God the Father and the Lord Jesus Christ, he actually means that the church is in the Triune God (1 Thes. 1:1; 1 Cor. 1:2; 12:4-6):

   a. The expressions *God the Father* and *the Lord Jesus Christ* both imply the Spirit; therefore, in 1 Thessalonians 1:1 the Spirit is implied and understood, and we may speak of the church being in the Triune God.

   b. According to the Bible, there is no such thing as the church being merely in God; rather, the church is in the processed Triune God (Matt. 28:19; 2 Cor. 13:14).

   c. For the church to be in God the Father and the Lord Jesus Christ means that the church is in the processed Triune God—the One who has become the life-

giving Spirit with the Father and the Son
(Matt. 28:19; Eph. 4:4-6; John 14:20).
2. If we see the vision of the church in the Triune God, this vision will control our thinking, our activities, and our entire life (Prov.
29:18a; Acts 26:19).

Morning Nourishment

Exo. ...Thus you shall say to the children of Israel, Jeho-
3:15-16 vah, the God of your fathers, the God of Abraham,
the God of Isaac, and the God of Jacob, has sent
me to you. This is My name forever, and this is My
memorial from generation to generation. Go, and
gather the elders of Israel together, and say to them,
Jehovah, the God of your fathers, the God of Abraham, of Isaac, and of Jacob, has appeared to me...

The book of Genesis reveals the complete Triune God of the
three sections of the life of a corporate person. Genesis does not
consider Abraham, Isaac, and Jacob as three separate persons
but as one complete corporate person with three sections.

Our God is the God of three particular persons—the God of
Abraham, the God of Isaac, and the God of Jacob. (*The History
of God in His Union with Man,* p. 133)

Today's Reading

The first beginning [that God's people had] was with Abraham because God's selection and calling began with Abraham.
The other beginning was with the nation of Israel....In between
these two beginnings, God gained three persons, Abraham,
Isaac, and Jacob....From that point on, the nation of Israel
became the people of God, and God had a people of His own....
Without Abraham, Isaac, and Jacob, there would not be the
nation of Israel, and without Abraham, Isaac, and Jacob, there
would not be a people of God.

The dealings which these three received before God and the
experiences they went through culminated in a people of God.
Hence, the total experiences of Abraham, Isaac, and Jacob are
the experiences that all of God's people should have. The
attainments of these three should be the attainments of all the
people of God....All the people of God should have the element
of Abraham, the element of Isaac, and the element of Jacob in
them. Without these elements, we cannot become God's people.
(*CWWN,* vol. 35, pp. 5-7)

As you read the book of Genesis, you will notice that the records of Adam, Abel, Enoch, and Noah are quite distinct one from another. The records of Abraham, Isaac, and Jacob, however, overlap. Genesis, speaking of them, considers them as one corporate man....The significance of this overlapping is that, according to the experience of life, these three persons are one man, a corporate man. (*Life-study of Genesis,* p. 516)

In the section of Abraham, we see God the Father who calls man, justifies man, and equips man to live by faith and live in fellowship with Him (Gen. 12:1; 15:6; ch. 17; ch. 18; 19:29; 21:1-13; 22:1-18). Genesis 12:1 shows us the Father's calling and 15:6 reveals His justification. Chapter 17 shows us how God equipped Abraham to live a life by faith. Then chapter 18 reveals how God made Abraham to live a life in fellowship with Him. It is a chapter of fellowship between God and His human friend, Abraham.

The section of Isaac represents God the Son, the second of the Triune God, who blesses man with the inheritance of all His riches, with a life of the enjoyment of His abundance, and with a life in peace (Gen. 25:5; 26:3-4, 12-33).

We see God the Father loving man and choosing man in the section of Jacob....Jacob is the last of the three, yet he is used by God to signify the Father in His loving and choosing man. Malachi 1:2 says that God loved Jacob, and Romans 9:10-13 says that God selected Jacob, choosing him even before he was born.

In the section of the life of Jacob with Joseph, we see God the Spirit who works in all things for the good of His lovers [cf. Rom. 8:28]....In the life of Jacob with Joseph, we see that the Spirit transforms man and makes man mature in the divine life that man may be able to bless all the people, to rule over all the earth, and to satisfy all the people with God the Son as the life supply (Gen. 27:41; 28:1—35:10; chs. 37; 39—49; Rom. 8:28-29). (*The History of God in His Union with Man,* pp. 134, 133, 134-135)

Further Reading: The History of God in His Union with Man, ch. 10;
    CWWN, vol. 35, "The God of Abraham, Isaac, and Jacob," ch. 1

Enlightenment and inspiration: _____
_____
_____
_____

Morning Nourishment

Rom.   (As it is written, "I have appointed you a father of
4:17   many nations") in the sight of God whom he be-
       lieved, who gives life to the dead and calls the
       things not being as being.
11:36 Because out from Him and through Him and to Him
       are all things. To Him be the glory forever. Amen.

In order to bring a group of people to come under His name,
and in order to make them His people, God did a special work in
three persons, Abraham, Isaac, and Jacob, respectively, and gave
each one of them particular experiences. God gave Abraham the
experience of knowing God as the Father, showing that everything comes from God. He gave Isaac the experience of knowing
the enjoyment of the Son, showing that everything the Son has
is from the Father. He gave Jacob the experience of the discipline
of the Holy Spirit to deal with his natural life and constitute
Christ into him. Abraham, Isaac, and Jacob are the beginning
of the history of God's people. As such, their total experience
should be the experience of all of God's people. (*CWWN,* vol. 35,
"The God of Abraham, Isaac, and Jacob," p. 3)

Today's Reading

Abraham believed God regarding two things: (1) the birth of
Isaac, which is related to the God who "calls the things not being
as being," and (2) the offering up and the gaining back of Isaac,
which is related to the God who "gives life to the dead." Abraham
believed such a God and applied Him to his situation. (Rom. 4:17,
footnote 1)

The source of faith is God. He is the One who calls things not
being as being and gives life to the dead (Rom. 4:17). (*Crystallization-study of the Epistle to the Romans,* p. 84)

God's goal must be achieved according to God's time and
through God's power....God's emphasis is not on whether something has happened, but on what the source is. Often our atten-
tion is just on the correctness of the results and the forms. Whatever we think is correct is taken to be correct, and whatever we

think is right is taken to be right. However, God is concerned with where something comes from and who is doing it.

God intended that Abraham be the father. Therefore, He did a special work on him in order to show him what it means for God to be the Father. For God to be the Father means that everything should issue from God. If Abraham did not see that everything issued from God and that He is the Father, he would not have been qualified to be the father of many nations. Yet the begetting of Ishmael issued from Abraham himself and was not from God.

God is the Father, and everything originates from Him. The day that God shows you that He is the Father will be a blessed day. On that day you will realize that you cannot do anything and that you are helpless. You will not have to try to hold yourself back from doing this thing or that thing. Instead you will ask, "Has God initiated this?" This is the experience of Abraham. His experience shows us that he had no thought of becoming God's people. Abraham did not initiate anything. It was God who initiated.

This was Abraham. God was the Initiator of everything for him; he had nothing to do with it. If you know that God is the Father, you will not be so confident and will not say that you can do whatever you want. You will only say, "If the Lord is willing, I will do this and that. Whatever the Lord says, I will do." This does not mean that you should be indecisive. It means that you truly do not know what to do and that you only know after the Father has revealed His will.

What is the lesson we learn from Isaac? Galatians 4 says that Isaac is the promised son (v. 23). In Isaac we see that everything comes from the Father. (*CWWN*, vol. 35, pp. 59, 54, 8-10)

Abraham's offering of his beloved and only son, Isaac, on the altar is a vivid picture of God the Father's offering of His beloved and only Son, Jesus Christ, on the cross. In this picture Isaac typifies Christ in a detailed way. (Gen. 22:2, footnote 1)

Further Reading: CWWN, vol. 35, "The God of Abraham, Isaac, and Jacob," chs. 6-7; *Life-study of Genesis*, msg. 38

Enlightenment and inspiration: _____

_____

_____

_____

Morning Nourishment

Gen. And Sarah my master's wife bore a son to my
24:36 master after she had become old. And he has given
all that he has to him.

1 Cor. For who distinguishes you? And what do you have
4:7 that you did not receive? And if you did receive *it*,
why do you boast as though not having received *it*?

Many people cannot be in the position of Abraham because
they cannot be in the position of Isaac....It is impossible to have
the experience of Abraham without the experience of Isaac. It is
also impossible to have the experience of Isaac without the experience of Abraham. We have to see that God is the Father and
that everything proceeds from Him. We also have to see that we
are sons and that everything we have is from Him. The life of the
Son which we inherit comes from Him. In the eyes of God we are
only those who receive. Salvation is received, victory is received,
justification is received, sanctification is received, forgiveness is
received, and freedom is received. The principle of receiving is
the principle of Isaac. We have to say, Hallelujah! Hallelujah!
Everything we have is from God. (*CWWN*, vol. 35, p. 10)

Today's Reading

Not only do we have to know God as the Father, but we have to
know Christ as the Son. What is the meaning of God as the Son?
It means that everything is received and nothing is initiated by
Him. In Abraham we see God's purpose. In Isaac we see God's
power. In Abraham we see the standard which God requires of
His people. In Isaac we see the life which enables God's people to
reach that standard. Many Christians have one basic problem:
They only see God's purpose but do not see God's provisions.
They see God's standard but do not see God's life. They see God's
demands, but do not see the power that meets these demands.
This is why we have to consider Isaac as well as Abraham.

Abraham shows us that everything is of God; we cannot do
anything by ourselves. Isaac shows us that everything comes
from God, and our place is to receive.

We can see Isaac's characteristics. Throughout his entire life, everything he had was a matter of enjoyment and receiving.... Knowing the God of Isaac means only one thing: knowing God as the Supplier and that everything comes from Him. If we want to know the Father, we have to know the Son. In order to know the God of Abraham, we have to know the God of Isaac. We are helpless if we only know the God of Abraham because He dwells in unapproachable light (1 Tim. 6:16). But thank the Lord that He is also the God of Isaac. This means that everything that Abraham had was Isaac's. It also means that everything comes by receiving.

What is the lesson we learn from Jacob? Abraham speaks to us of the Father, Isaac speaks to us of the Son, and Jacob speaks to us of the Holy Spirit. It does not mean that Jacob represents the Holy Spirit, but that his experiences represent the work of the Holy Spirit. Jacob's history is a type of the discipline of the Holy Spirit. (*CWWN*, vol. 35, pp. 91, 13, 93, 12)

Eventually, the Bible says that God is the God of Abraham, the God of Isaac, and the God of Jacob, and that this God is not the God of the dead but of the living (Matt. 22:32). My God is not only the God of Abraham and the God of Isaac; He is also the God of Jacob, the God of dealings who deals with me all day long. (*Life-study of Genesis,* pp. 896-897)

The title *the God of Jacob* implies how the Holy Spirit disciplined Jacob, how He dealt with Jacob's natural life, how He constituted Christ into Jacob, and how He bore the fruit of the Spirit in Jacob. If we want to know the God of Jacob, we have to know the constitution by the Spirit and the fruit of the Spirit. If we want to know the God of Jacob, we need to allow the Spirit to perform His work in us, to deal with our natural life, to constitute Christ into our inward being, and to bring forth the fruit of the Spirit in us so that we can become the vessels of God's testimony. (*CWWN,* vol. 35, "The God of Abraham, Isaac, and Jacob," p. 171)

Further Reading: CWWN, vol. 35, "The God of Abraham, Isaac, and Jacob," chs. 4-5

Enlightenment and inspiration: _____

_____

_____

_____

Morning Nourishment

Heb. **Now no discipline at the present time seems to be**
12:11 ***a matter* of joy, but of grief; but afterward it yields**
the peaceable fruit of righteousness to those who
have been exercised by it.
Rom. **And we know that all things work together for**
8:28 **good to those who love God, to those who are**
called according to *His* purpose.

Some brothers and sisters are exceptionally clever, thought-
ful, shrewd, calculating, and resourceful. But we must remember that we do not walk in fleshly wisdom but in the grace of
God (2 Cor. 1:12). Jacob experienced the continual discipline of
the Holy Spirit. As a result, his cleverness was never able to
have its way. (*CWWN*, vol. 35, "The God of Abraham, Isaac, and
Jacob," p. 12)

Today's Reading

The discipline of the Holy Spirit that we are now considering does not refer to the inward discipline of the Holy Spirit, for
that is the function of the Holy Spirit within us as the anoint-
ing. The discipline of the Holy Spirit refers to what the Holy
Spirit is doing in our outward environment; it refers to His
arranging of all people, things, and happenings, through which
we are being disciplined.

Normally, the more a person is disciplined by the Holy
Spirit, the more he is terminated. The end result of the discipline of the Holy Spirit is always that we may be torn down,
broken, and reduced to nothing. It is through the discipline of
the Holy Spirit that God completely tears down our old creation so that the element of His new creation may be built up in
us. (*The Experience of Life*, pp. 259, 266)

God has given Christ to the believers; this is the first
step. But He wants to do a deeper work, which is to have Christ
formed in us [Gal. 4:19]. God deals with our natural life so that
Christ may be formed in us, that is, that Christ may be wrought
into us and constituted in us. (*CWWN*, vol. 35, "The God of

Abraham, Isaac, and Jacob," pp. 173-174)

The God of Abraham, Isaac, and Jacob is *Jehovah Elohim* (Gen. 2:4-22; Exo. 3:15).…*Elohim* means "the faithful mighty One." God is faithful and mighty. *Jehovah* means "He who was, who is, and who is to be." Genesis 2:4-22 repeatedly mentions Jehovah Elohim, a divine title indicating God's relationship with His elect.

Jehovah as the great I Am is the self-existing and ever-existing Triune God (Exo. 3:13-14). He is self-existing, without beginning, and ever-existing, without ending. The beginning and ending in the whole universe is God [Rev. 22:13].

The God of Abraham, Isaac, and Jacob is the God of the tabernacle.…Abraham, Isaac, and Jacob each lived in a tent (Gen. 12:8; 13:18; 18:1; 26:17, 25; 33:18; 35:21; Heb. 11:9). It is significant that the Bible does not say that Joseph lived in a tent. This shows that Joseph was a part of the life of Jacob. While Abraham, Isaac, and Jacob were living in tents, they were eagerly waiting for the eternal tabernacle of God, the city of New Jerusalem (Heb. 11:10; Rev. 21:2-3). The tent in which they lived was a type of the New Jerusalem as the coming reality, the eternal tent. They were living in a type, eagerly waiting for the reality, the New Jerusalem. (*The History of God in His Union with Man,* pp. 132, 140)

When God first met Jacob, He said, "I am Jehovah, the God of Abraham your father and the God of Isaac" (Gen. 28:13). This implied that God was to be Jacob's God. We all have experienced the God of Abraham and the God of Isaac. Since the God of Abraham is the God of justification and the God of Isaac is the God of grace, this means that we have experienced the God of justification and the God of grace. Although we have experienced such a God, we also need to meet and experience the God of Jacob. This means that God will be to us the God of transformation, the God of dealings. (*Life-study of Genesis,* p. 896)

Further Reading: The History of God in His Union with Man, ch. 11; *Life-study of Genesis,* msg. 69; *The Experience of Life,* ch. 12

Enlightenment and inspiration: _____

_____

_____

_____

Morning Nourishment

Gal. **For neither is circumcision anything nor uncir-**
6:15-16 **cumcision, but a new creation** *is what matters.* **And**
as many as walk by this rule, peace be upon them
and mercy, even upon the Israel of God.

The real Israel (Rom. 9:6b; 2:28-29; Phil. 3:3), [includes] all
the Gentile and Jewish believers in Christ, who are the true sons
of Abraham (Gal. 3:7, 29), who are the household of the faith
(6:10), and who are those in the new creation. They walk by "this
rule," express God's image, and execute God's authority, and are
typified by Jacob, who was transformed into Israel, a prince of
God and a victor (Gen. 32:27-28). (Gal. 6:16, footnote 4)

Today's Reading

Paul concludes Galatians 6:16 with the words *even upon the Is-*
rael of God. The Greek word rendered "even" (*kai*) here is not con-
nective but explicative, indicating that the apostle considers the
many individual believers in Christ collectively the Israel of God.

As sons of God [3:26], we are His folks, members of His household. But God's New Testament economy is not only to make us
His sons, but also to make us the Israel of God.

On the one hand we are sons of God, members of the divine
family. On the other hand, we are kings-to-be, those destined to
be kings. Kingship is related to the Israel of God....To be kings,
the Israel of God, we need another kind of living, a particular walk
by the Spirit. We need both the living of sons of God and that of
the Israel of God.

We, the sons of God, are the true Israel, for we are God's household, His chosen people today. We may not be Israel outwardly, but
we are Israel inwardly. This is why we say that we, the believers in
Christ, are the true Israel. The outward nation of Israel has little
concern for God. However, we have a genuine concern for God and
speak of Him continually. We are indeed the Israel of God.

In a sense, the nation of Israel is the Israel of God and a testimony of God, even though many Israelites are rebellious and
very sinful. However, the real Israel, the spiritual Israel, is the

church. But because both the nation of Israel and the church are in a low condition, there is the need for the Lord to recover the real Israel of God. For such a recovery, we need two kinds of living, two kinds of walk. In the first walk we shall have such virtues as love, joy, peace, meekness, and longsuffering, all of which are the expression of the Christ who lives in us. We also need the second kind of walk so that we may be the Israel of God bearing God's kingship, representing Him with His authority, and executing His governmental administration.

These two kinds of walks are illustrated by our life as citizens of the United States. On the one hand, we are persons living in an ordinary way; on the other hand, we are citizens of this nation. As persons, we need to be loving, peaceful, joyful, faithful, and meek. However, in order for the United States to remain a strong nation, we also need to live as good citizens, fulfilling all the requirements of the government. As citizens, we need to pay taxes, serve in the army, and fulfill other obligations. Spiritually speaking, we are both the sons of God and the Israel of God. As sons of God, we need to be loving, joyful, peaceful, faithful, and meek. As the Israel of God, we must walk according to the elementary rules of God's New Testament economy.

Praise the Lord that we are now sons of God! As God's sons, we need a walk by the Spirit to express Christ in all His virtues. We also need another kind of walk by the Spirit, the walk according to certain rules or principles, leading toward the goal for the fulfillment of God's purpose. If we have the second kind of walk by the Spirit, we shall be not only sons of God, but also a new creation and the Israel of God. We need to live the new creation and as the new Israel of God. In order to live a new creation and live as the Israel of God, we need the second kind of walk. We need to walk orderly according to the elementary principles of God's economy. (*Life-study of Galatians,* pp. 269, 380-381, 269, 381-382, 373-374)

Further Reading: Life-study of Galatians, msgs. 30, 42-43

Enlightenment and inspiration: _____

_____

_____

_____

Morning Nourishment

1 Thes. **Paul and Silvanus and Timothy to the church of**
1:1 **the Thessalonians in God the Father and the Lord**
    Jesus Christ: Grace to you and peace.
Matt. **Go therefore and disciple all the nations, baptizing**
28:19 **them into the name of the Father and of the Son**
    and of the Holy Spirit.

When Paul speaks of the church of the Thessalonians in God
the Father and the Lord Jesus Christ, he actually means that
the church of the Thessalonians is in the Triune God. Paul's
word concerning the Father and the Lord Jesus Christ indicates
or implies that God is triune. If God were not triune, how could
He be the Father and the Son? It would be impossible. Furthermore, Paul's reference to the Father and Christ also implies the
Holy Spirit....Elsewhere in this chapter Paul explicitly speaks of
the Holy Spirit. Therefore, 1 Thessalonians 1 clearly shows the
Triune God—the Father, the Son, and the Holy Spirit. Both
1 Thessalonians 1:1 and 2 Thessalonians 1:1 reveal that the
church is composed of a group of sinners who have been saved
and regenerated and who are now in the Triune God. How wonderful! (*Life-study of 1 Thessalonians,* p. 46)

Today's Reading

Both in 1 and 2 Thessalonians the location of the church is
not a city—it is God. Furthermore, the church is in the Triune
God. This is indicated by the fact that Paul says "in God the
Father and the Lord Jesus Christ." The object of the preposition
in is both God the Father and the Lord Jesus Christ. The Father
and the Son are two and yet are one. For the church to be in God
the Father and the Lord Jesus Christ means that the church is
in the Triune God.

Be assured that the very God spoken of in 1 Thessalonians
1:1 is the Triune God. We know this by the fact that Paul first
mentions the Father, the first of the Trinity. Whenever we have
the first, we also have the second, the Son, and also the third, the
Spirit. The very fact that Paul speaks of the Father is a strong

indication that he is thinking of the Triune God....The expressions *God the Father* and *the Lord Jesus Christ* both imply the Spirit. Therefore, in 1:1 the Spirit is implied and understood.

It is a rather simple matter to say that the church is of God or of Christ. But it is deeper and more profound to declare that the church is in God the Father and in the Lord Jesus Christ. For example, it is one thing to say that we are of a particular person. However, it is altogether another matter to claim to be in that person. Humanly speaking, it is possible to be of someone, but it is not possible to be literally in that one. Only in a way that is organic and of life can the church be in the Triune God. We do not adequately understand the way of life, but God does understand it in full. Furthermore, only God can do something in the way of life. In a way that is organic and of life, God has made it possible for the church to be in the Triune God.

Now we need to consider carefully the difference between God and the Triune God. To speak only of God is to regard Him as if He had not been processed. However, the Triune God denotes God in His process.

This Triune God is the processed God. He has passed through the process of incarnation, human living, crucifixion, and resurrection. In crucifixion, He accomplished redemption, the termination of the old creation, and the destruction of Satan and death. In resurrection, He germinated the new creation. Now He is the life-giving Spirit as the ultimate consummation of the Triune God. The church is in such a Triune God. The church is in the processed Triune God, the One who has become the life-giving Spirit with the Father and the Son.

I have the full assurance that if you see what is covered in these messages on the church in the Triune God, you will be different both in your concept and in your activity. These messages convey a vision, a vision that will control our thinking, our activities, and our entire life. (*Life-study of 1 Thessalonians,* pp. 22, 58-62, 68)

Further Reading: Life-study of 1 Thessalonians, msgs. 1, 3-5, 7-11

Enlightenment and inspiration: _____

_____

_____

_____

Hymns, #608

1   What mystery, the Father, Son, and Spirit,
       In person three, in substance all are one.
     How glorious, this God our being enters
       To be our all, thru Spirit in the Son!

           The Triune God has now become our all!
             How wonderful! How glorious!
           This Gift divine we never can exhaust!
             How excellent! How marvelous!

2   How rich the source, the Father as the fountain,
       And all this wealth He wants man to enjoy!
     O blessed fact, this vast exhaustless portion
       Is now for us forever to employ!

3   How wonderful, the Son is God's expression
       Come in the flesh to dwell with all mankind!
     Redemption's work, how perfectly effective,
       That sinners we with God might oneness find.

4   The Spirit is the Son's transfiguration
       Come into us as life the full supply.
     Amazing fact, our spirit with the Spirit
       Now mingles and in oneness joins thereby!

5   How real it is that God is now the Spirit
       For us to touch, experience day by day!
     Astounding fact, with God we are one spirit,
       And differ not in life in any way!

Composition for prophecy with main point and sub-points: _____

_____
_____
_____
_____
_____
_____
_____
_____
_____
_____
_____
_____
_____
_____
_____
_____
_____
_____
_____
_____
_____
_____
_____
_____
_____
_____
_____
_____
_____
_____
_____
_____
_____
_____
_____
_____

Living by Faith—
Being Today's River Crossers
to Live the Life of the Altar and the Tent

Scripture Reading: Josh. 24:2-3; Acts 7:2; Heb. 11:8-10; Gen. 12:1-3, 7-8; 13:3-4, 18

Day 1 I. **As believers in Christ, we are the corporate seed of Abraham, repeating the history of Abraham (Rom. 4:11-12):**
   A. Christ as the life-giving Spirit is the transfigured seed (descendant, or son) of Abraham dispensed into us to make us the sons of Abraham and the corporate seed of Abraham (1 Cor. 15:45; Gal. 3:6-7, 9, 16, 29).
   B. Abraham's living by faith is presently being repeated among us (Heb. 11:6).
   C. The Christian life and the church life today are the harvest of the life and history of Abraham (Rom. 4:12).

II. **The first Hebrew was Abraham, the father of all those who contact God by faith; therefore, God is called "the God of the Hebrews" (Gen. 14:13; Exo. 7:16; 9:1, 13; Rom. 4:11-12; Heb. 1:1):**
   A. The root of the word *Hebrew* means "to pass over"; it can mean specifically to pass over a river, that is, to pass over from this side of the river to the other side; therefore, a Hebrew is a river crosser (Gen. 14:13):
      1. River crossers are a people separated from the world.
      2. Abraham left Chaldea, crossed the river, and came into Canaan, the good land of blessing (Josh. 24:2-3).
Day 2 B. Abraham's crossing the river and entering into the new land signifies his entering into an uplifted, new mankind, which would be used by God to be His expression:

    1. We need to leave the law and cross over to grace (Heb. 4:16; 7:18-19; 12:28; 13:9).

    2. We need to leave the old covenant and cross over to the new covenant (8:6-7, 13).

    3. We need to leave the ritualistic service of the Old Testament and cross over to the spiritual reality of the New Testament (Heb. 8:5; 9:9-14).

    4. We need to leave Judaism and cross over to the church (13:13; 10:25).

    5. We need to leave the earthly things and cross over to the heavenly things (12:18-24).

    6. We need to leave the outer court, where the altar is, and cross over to the Holy of Holies, where God is (13:9-10; 10:19-20).

    7. We need to leave the soul and cross over to the spirit (4:12).

    8. We need to leave the beginning of truth and life and cross over to the maturity of life in the truth (5:11—6:1).

C. Apparently, Abraham journeyed into Canaan (Gen. 12:4-5), but actually, the God of glory appeared to him (Acts 7:2-3) and then "removed him" across the Euphrates River into the good land (v. 4; Josh. 24:2-3).

Day 3 **III. If we would walk in the steps of Abraham's faith, we must be those who live the life of the altar and the tent, taking Christ as our life and the church as our living to live a life of being transfused by God, consecrating our all to God, and taking His presence as our road map (Rom. 4:11-12; Gal. 3:6-9; Heb. 11:9; Gen. 12:7-8; 13:3-4, 18):**

A. The Lord Jesus appeared to Abraham as the great I Am, the God of glory, to transfuse Himself into Abraham (John 8:56-58; Exo. 3:14-15; Acts 7:2).

B. We need to come again and again to the Lord and beseech Him:

1. We must pray, "Appear to me again and again, and speak to me again and again!"
2. We need to have a continuous seeing, an eternal seeing, of what the goal of God is (John 14:21; Acts 26:16; 2 Tim. 4:8).

C. God's goal with Abraham was not merely to save him out of his environment and his background but to bring him into the land of Canaan for the fulfillment of God's purpose; likewise, God's goal with the New Testament believers is not merely to save them from their fallen condition but to bring them into the reality of the good land, which is the all-inclusive Christ as the portion allotted by God to all the called ones (Gen. 12:5; Deut. 8:7-10; Col. 1:12; 2:6-7).

D. Through His repeated appearings to Abraham, God transfused Himself into him, causing him to experience a spiritual infusion with a spiritual infiltration of God's essence into his being (Gen. 12:1-3, 7-8; 13:14-17; 15:1-7; Rom. 4:3; Gen. 18:17-19; cf. Acts 26:16; 22:14-15).

E. God's appearing and transfusing issue in our living by faith for His perfect will to build up the church as the Body of Christ, consummating in the New Jerusalem (Gen. 12:7-8; 13:3-4, 18; Rom. 1:17; 4:16-17; Heb. 12:1-2a; Matt. 16:18; Rom. 12:1-2; Rev. 21:2).

F. Abraham's faith did not originate with himself; rather, his believing in God was a reaction to the God of glory appearing to him and to the transfusing and infusing of God's element into his being (Acts 7:2).

Day 4

G. God's appearing and transfusing issue in our consecration, causing us to build an altar, live in a tent, and live totally for God; by God's appearing and transfusing, Abraham trusted in God for His instant leading, taking God's presence as the road map for his traveling (Gen. 12:7-8; 13:3-4, 18; Heb. 11:8):

1. When we meet God Himself, we have the power to deny ourselves.
2. The matter of denying the self ceases to be optional when we have met God—no man can see God and live.

H. An altar is for worshipping God by offering all that we are and have to God for His purpose; building an altar means that our life is for God, that God is our life, and that the meaning of our life is God (Gen. 8:20-21a; Exo. 29:18-22).

Day 5   IV. **Abraham built three altars in three places— Shechem, Bethel, and Hebron; these three places represent the good land, typifying the all-inclusive Christ as the all-inclusive Spirit (Col. 1:12; 2:6-7; Phil. 1:19):**

A. "Abram passed through the land to the place of Shechem, to the oak of Moreh...And Jehovah appeared to Abram and said, To your seed I will give this land. And there he built an altar to Jehovah who had appeared to him" (Gen. 12:6-7):

1. *Shechem* means "shoulder"—the place of strength; the name *Moreh* means "teacher" or "teaching"; Abraham journeyed to a land where he could receive God as his power and where he could know God as we do today through the healthy teaching of God's economy (Phil. 3:10; 1 Tim. 1:3-6; 6:3).

2. The power of the good land is the power of life that satisfies man, the power of the flowing Triune God to know Christ inwardly, so that we may become and build up the New Jerusalem (John 4:14b; Psa. 84:3, 5-7, 11).

B. "And he proceeded from there to the mountain on the east of Bethel and pitched his tent, with Bethel on the west and Ai on the east; and there he built an altar to Jehovah and called upon the name of Jehovah" (Gen. 12:8):

1. *Bethel* means "house of God," and *Ai* means "a heap of ruins"; in the eyes of the called

ones, only Bethel—the church life, the Body
life—is worthwhile; everything else is a
heap of ruins (cf. Eph. 1:10).

2. The desolate heap includes our natural life;
only after our natural life has been dealt with
by God, and only after we have been subdued
to realize that the natural life should be
judged rather than praised, will we be joined
spontaneously to the brothers and sisters to
live out the life of the Body of Christ (Phil. 3:3;
Gal. 6:3, 14-15; 2 Cor. 12:7-9).

Day 6   C. "And Abram moved his tent and came and dwelt
by the oaks of Mamre, which are in Hebron, and
there he built an altar to Jehovah" (Gen. 13:18):

1. *Hebron* means "fellowship," "communion,"
or "friendship"; *Mamre* means "strength" or
"fatness" with riches for transfusion, infusion, saturation, and permeation by the
sealing Spirit (Eph. 1:13-14).

2. Abraham had his failures, and there was
the forsaking of the altar and the tent; however, with him there was a recovery, and
recovery is a matter of returning to the
altar and the tent with calling on the name of
the Lord (Gen. 12:9-10; 13:3-4; Rom. 10:12-13;
12:1-2).

3. Eventually, at Hebron Abraham's tent became a place where he had fellowship with
God and where God could fellowship with
him (Gen. 13:18).

4. If we have seen the house of God, the church
as the Body of Christ, we will do everything
in fellowship with God and with one another
(1 John 1:3).

5. At Hebron God was revealed to Abraham as
the God in His human friendship so that He
might gain him to be His intercessor for
the rescue of His backslidden believer, for the
bringing forth of Christ, and for the destruc-

tion of the works of the devil in His chosen
people (James 2:23; 2 Chron. 20:7; Isa. 41:8;
Gen. 18; 1 John 5:16a; Gal. 4:19; 1 John 3:8).

V. **Abraham's dwelling in a tent, a movable abode,
    testifies that he did not belong to the world
    but lived the life of a sojourner on earth;
    erecting a tent is an expression, a declara-
    tion, that we do not belong to this world but
    that we belong to a better country, the New
    Jerusalem (Heb. 11:9-10, 13-16; cf. Psa. 90:1):**

A. By living the life of the altar and the tent, Abra-
    ham bore God's testimony, God's expression (Gen.
    12:1-3; Exo. 25:22; 38:21):

    1. All the things we possess must pass through
        the altar; they are given back to us by the
        Lord to meet our need in the world.

    2. We may use them, but they must not govern
        us; we can have them and let them go; they
        can be given, and they can be taken away—
        this is the principle of the tent life.

B. God's purpose in choosing His people is for them
    to become His testimony, a great and holy na-
    tion; God's goal is to gain a group of people who
    will declare, "I belong to Jehovah; I am the
    Lord's" (1 Pet. 2:9; Rom. 14:7-9).

C. Abraham's tent with the altar built by him was
    a prefigure of the Tabernacle of the Testimony
    with the altar built by the children of Israel
    (Exo. 38:21).

D. Abraham's tent was a miniature of the New Jeru-
    salem, the ultimate tent, the ultimate tabernacle
    of God (Gen. 9:26-27; John 1:14; Rev. 21:2-3).

E. As we are living in the "tent" of the church life,
    we are waiting for its ultimate consummation—
    the ultimate Tent of Meeting, the New Jeru-
    salem (1 Tim. 3:15; Lev. 1:1; Heb. 11:9-10; cf. Lev.
    23:39-43).

Morning Nourishment

Rom. And the father of circumcision to those...who also
4:12 walk in the steps of that faith of our father Abraham, which *he had* in uncircumcision.

Gal. Know then that they who are of faith, these are
3:7 sons of Abraham.

14 In order that the blessing of Abraham might come
to the Gentiles in Christ Jesus, that we might
receive the promise of the Spirit through faith.

The seed of Abraham is for the believers in Christ, who are
Abraham's seed, to inherit the consummated Spirit, the consummation of the processed Triune God, as their divine inheritance—
their spiritual blessing for eternity (Acts 26:18; Eph. 1:14a; Gal.
3:14). Christ is the seed of Abraham, and all His believers are
also the seed of Abraham (v. 29)....Abraham is our father (Rom.
4:12). (*The Central Line of the Divine Revelation,* pp. 88-89)

Today we are repeating the life and history of Abraham.
Once there was only one Abraham; now there are many. The
church life today is the harvest of the life and history of Abraham. Abraham's life by faith is presently being repeated among
us. We all are here building an altar and pitching a tent. Look at
the church life: we have an altar and a real tabernacle. This is a
picture of the coming New Jerusalem where we shall spend
eternity with God. (*Life-study of Genesis,* p. 563)

Today's Reading

The word *Hebrew* was first used in Genesis 14:13, at the time
when Abraham was about to fight for the rescue of his nephew
Lot....Abraham was a Hebrew. As a result of considerable study,
we discovered that the root of the word *Hebrew* means "to pass
over." It especially means to pass over a river from one region to another and from one side to another. Therefore, the word *Hebrew*
means a crosser, a river crosser, one who crosses a river. Abraham
was a river crosser. He crossed that great flood (Josh. 24:2-3).

Abraham was born in Chaldea, the site of ancient Babylon,
Babel. Between Chaldea and the good land of Canaan was a

great river flowing from north to south. This is very meaningful. All things, including the land, were created by God to fulfill His purpose. The land of Chaldea became satanic, devilish, and demonic. It was a land filled with idols, a land totally usurped by God's enemy and possessed by the evil one. So God intervened to call Abraham out of that idolatrous land, out of that land which had been usurped, possessed, poisoned, corrupted, and ruined by Satan. God simply called Abraham out without telling him where he should go (Heb. 11:8). Abraham had to look to the Lord step by step, saying to Him, "Lord, where should I go?" Abraham knew what he had to leave, but he did not know where he was to go. Eventually God led him to that great river, and Abraham crossed it. Joshua 24:2-3 says that Abraham "dwelt across the River" and that the Lord took him "from across the River and brought him throughout all the land of Canaan." Therefore, a Hebrew is a person from the other side of the water.

Now we can understand the real meaning of baptism. Why must all repentant people be baptized? Because the world in which we are has been usurped, possessed, corrupted, and ruined by God's enemy. It is no longer good for the fulfillment of God's purpose. God's salvation is not merely to rescue us from hell to heaven. God's salvation is to bring us out of the land that has been possessed and ruined by Satan. How can we pass out of it? By being baptized. Every baptistery is a great river, a great flood. After you have been baptized, you come out on the other shore....We must all declare, "We are Hebrews! We are typical Hebrews."...We are the true, genuine Hebrews because we have passed over the river. Everyone among us is a real river crosser.... We are people who have crossed over from the other side. What is for us on this side? Churching! We are the water crossers. We are Hebrews. The water has separated us....Now we, today's Hebrews, are building the church. (*Life-study of Hebrews,* pp. 2-5)

Further Reading: Life-study of Hebrews, msg. 1; *The Central Line of the Divine Revelation,* msg. 8

Enlightenment and inspiration: _____

_____

_____

_____

Morning Nourishment

Heb. Let us therefore come forward with boldness to
4:16 the throne of grace that we may receive mercy and
      find grace for timely help.
13:13 Let us therefore go forth unto Him outside the
      camp, bearing His reproach.
6:1 ...Let us be brought on to maturity, not laying
      again a foundation of repentance from dead works
      and of faith in God.

Although God created man with such an intention and purpose, man has been ruined and corrupted....The Bible often uses
lands and cities as figures to symbolize man. So Chaldea and Babylon signify the ruined and corrupted man filled with idolatry.
Since man has fallen, there is the need to cross the river out of
the corrupted land into the elevated, new land, that is, into an
elevated, new mankind. So God came in and called Abraham out
of that ruined mankind, that is, out of Chaldea, making him the
head and father of the called race. Abraham crossed the river
and became the first Hebrew, the first river crosser. Abraham's
crossing the river and entering into the new land signified his
entering into an uplifted, new mankind which is to be used by
God to be His expression. (*Life-study of Hebrews,* p. 110)

Today's Reading

From Chaldea, the land of idolatry, which was on the other
side of the great river Euphrates, Abraham crossed over to
Canaan, the land of the worship of God, which was on this side of
the Euphrates (Josh. 24:2-3). The intention of God's speaking in
Hebrews was that the Jews who believed in the Lord but still lin-
gered in Judaism would leave the law and cross over to grace
(4:16; 7:18-19; 12:28; 13:9), that they would leave the old covenant and cross over to the new covenant (8:6-7, 13), and that they
would leave the ritualistic service of the Old Testament and
cross over to the spiritual reality of the New Testament (8:5; 9:9-
14); that is, that they would leave Judaism and cross over to the
church (13:13; 10:25), that they would leave the earthly things

and cross over to the heavenly things (12:18-24), that they would leave the outer court, where the altar is, and cross over to the Holiest of all, where God is (13:9-10; 10:19-20), that they would leave the soul and cross over to the spirit (4:12), and that they would leave the beginning of truth and life and cross over to the maturity of life in the truth (5:11—6:1). (Heb. 1:1, footnote 2)

We all must see that to be saved means to be called to fulfill God's purpose. To be saved is to be delivered out of many negative situations so that we may come into God's goal. Many Christians have been saved, but they have never come into God's goal. God's goal firstly is Christ. We are in Christ. We are in the enjoyment of Christ. This is God's good land. Secondly, God's goal is the church. Years ago I did not realize that, in a sense, the church is also the good land of Canaan. Furthermore, God's New Testament economy, the kingdom, and the Sabbath rest are all the good land to us today.

Regardless of how long Abraham delayed in answering God's calling, he could not delay God very long. According to God's feeling, a thousand years are the same as a day. Can you delay God a thousand years? No one can do this. At the most, we might delay him for fifty years, which in God's eyes are a little more than an hour. God is sovereign and patient....God is God. No one can frustrate Him. Once He has chosen and called you, He will not be stopped by anything. Sooner or later He will get through.... According to Acts 7:4, it was not Abraham who entered into the good land but God who removed him into the land. Although Hebrews 11:8 says that Abraham went out by faith, Acts 7:4 says that God removed him from Haran into Canaan. At most, we can delay the Lord for just a short time. Eventually we shall be gained by Him. If we delay, we shall only waste our time. God told Abraham to get out of his country. Since he did not do it in a rapid and clean-cut way, God removed him into His land. (*Life-study of Genesis*, pp. 546-547)

Further Reading: Life-study of Genesis, msgs. 39-40

Enlightenment and inspiration: _____

_____

_____

_____

Morning Nourishment

Acts   ...The God of glory appeared to our father Abra-
7:2   ham while he was in Mesopotamia...
John   Jesus said to them, Truly, truly, I say to you, Before
8:58   Abraham came into being, I am.
Heb.   By faith Abraham, being called, obeyed to go out unto
11:8   a place which he was to receive as an inheritance;
and he went out, not knowing where he was going.

[The glory in Acts 7:2] might have been visible glory (cf. v. 55), as when the cloud and the fire appeared to Israel (Exo. 16:10; 24:16-17; Lev. 9:23; Num. 14:10; 16:19; 20:6; Deut. 5:24) and filled the tabernacle and the temple (Exo. 40:35; 1 Kings 8:11). It was the God of such glory who appeared to Abraham and called him. His glory was a great attraction to him. It separated (sanctified) him from the world unto God (Exo. 29:43) and was a great encouragement and strength that enabled him to follow God (Gen. 12:1, 4). In the same principle, God calls the New Testament believers by His invisible glory (2 Pet. 1:3). (Acts 7:2, footnote 2)

[Not knowing where he was going] afforded Abraham constant opportunity to exercise his faith to trust in God for His instant leading, taking God's presence as the map for his traveling. (Heb. 11:8, footnote 1)

Today's Reading

Even if we are consciously trying to be a proper Christian, it is still possible for us to lose our vision. We can lose our vision even while we are working diligently day after day....If we do not live continuously in God's appearing, it will be easy for us to lose the vision of our calling. The calling that the church has received is the same as the calling that Abraham received. But many people have not seen the hope of this calling. Therefore, Paul prayed, "That you may know what is the hope of His calling" (Eph. 1:18). *Hope* indicates the content of this calling, the things included in God's calling. May God deliver us from selfish thoughts. We know that God calls us with a definite goal. Our salvation is to fulfill this goal. If we have not seen the substance of Abraham's calling, we will not see the meaning of our own calling. If we have not seen the key to Abraham's calling, we will not see our own ministry. If we do not see this, we will be like those who build a house without a foundation. How easy it is for us to forget what God wants to do! Many times, when we have too much to do and the work becomes a little more hectic, we lose sight of our spiritual calling. We need to come again and again to the Lord and beseech Him: "Appear to me again and again, and speak to me again and again!" We need to have a continuous seeing, an eternal seeing; we need to see God's goal and what God is doing. (*CWWN*, vol. 35, pp. 29-30)

God's goal with Abraham was not merely to save him out of his environment and his background but to bring him into the land of Canaan for the fulfillment of God's purpose. Likewise, God's goal with the New Testament believers is not merely to save them from their fallen condition but to bring them into the reality of the good land, which is the all-inclusive Christ as the portion allotted by God to all the called ones. (Gen. 12:5, footnote 3)

Abraham's faith did not come from his natural ability and it did not originate with himself. His believing in God was a reaction..., a response to the divine infusion....Genuine faith is the working of God within us. This is why God counted Abraham's faith as righteousness. It seemed that God was saying, "This faith is something of Me. It corresponds to Me. This is Abraham's righteousness before Me." What was that righteousness? It was the righteousness of God.

Whenever we preach the gospel of Jesus Christ in a normal way, there will be an appearing of the living Christ, and this appearing will transfuse Christ into people. I can confirm this by my own experience....My reaction to God was my believing in Him. That was my faith. God's reaction back to me was to justify me, to give His righteousness with peace and joy to me. (*Life-study of Romans*, pp. 94, 92)

Further Reading: CWWN, vol. 35, "The God of Abraham, Isaac, and Jacob," ch. 2; *Life-study of Romans*, msg. 8

Enlightenment and inspiration: _____

_____
_____
_____

Morning Nourishment

Gen. **And Jehovah appeared to Abram and said, To your**
12:7 **seed I will give this land. And there he built an**
     altar to Jehovah who had appeared to him.
13:3-4 **And he continued on his journey from the Negev as**
     far as Bethel, to the place where his tent had been at
     the beginning, between Bethel and Ai, to the place
     of the altar, which he had made there formerly; and
     there Abram called on the name of Jehovah.

In Genesis 12:7 we see that the altar is based on God's appearance. Where there is no divine appearance, there is no altar. No one can offer himself to God unless he has first met God....Consecration is not the result of man's exhortation or persuasion but of God's revelation. No one can voluntarily offer up all he has on the altar if God has not first appeared to him. By nature, no one can offer himself to God. Even when a man does want to offer himself to God, he finds that he really has nothing to offer. Some have said, "I want to give my heart to the Lord, but my heart will not agree." Man cannot come over to God's side. However, when man meets God, consecration takes place spontaneously in his life. If you catch sight of God just once and touch God just once, you are no longer your own. God is Someone who cannot be touched lightly! Once a man touches God, he can no longer live for himself. (*CWWN,* vol. 37, "The Life of the Altar and the Tent," p. 89)

Today's Reading

A turning point in our spiritual life does not come through our decision to do something for God; it does not come as a result of our resolving to do this or that for God. It comes when we see Him. When we meet God, a radical change takes place in our life. We can no longer do what we did in the past. When we meet God Himself, we have the power to deny ourselves. The matter of denying one's self ceases to be optional when we have met God. His appearance makes a person unable to go on by himself; it forces him to not live by himself anymore. God's appearance brings with it inexhaustible power. Such an appearance will alter the whole course of a person's life. For a Christian, the power to live for God is based on his vision of God. Oh! It is not our decision to serve the Lord that enables us to serve Him. It is not our will to build an altar that produces an altar. An altar is built when God comes to a man.

God appeared to Abraham, and Abraham built an altar. This altar was not for a sin offering but for a burnt offering. A sin offering is for redemption, while a burnt offering is an offering of ourselves to God.

God appeared to Abraham, and Abraham offered himself to God. Once a man sees God, he will offer himself up totally to God. It is impossible for a man to see God and yet be indifferent. The altar is present as soon as a person sees God. Once there is the taste of His grace, the result is the altar. Once a man sees God's mercy, he becomes a living sacrifice. When the Lord's light comes, he will say, "What shall I do, Lord?"

Abraham had not heard many doctrines about consecration, nor had he been urged by others to consecrate himself. But Abraham had seen God, and when he did, he immediately built an altar to God. O brothers and sisters, consecration is a spontaneous thing. Anyone to whom God has manifested Himself cannot do anything other than live for Him. Once God appears to a person, he will live totally for God. So it was with Abraham, and so it has been with everyone who has met God throughout the two thousand years of church history. (*CWWN,* vol. 37, pp. 90-92)

An altar means that we do not keep anything for ourselves. An altar means that we realize that we are here on earth for God. An altar means that our life is for God, that God is our life, and that the meaning of our life is God. So we put everything on the altar. We are not here making a name for ourselves; we are putting everything on the altar for the sake of His name. (*Life-study of Genesis,* p. 556)

Further Reading: CWWN, vol. 37, "The Life of the Altar and the Tent," ch. 16

Enlightenment and inspiration: _____

_____

_____

_____

Morning Nourishment

Gen. And Abram passed through the land to the place of
12:6-8 Shechem, to the oak of Moreh....And Jehovah appeared to Abram....And there he built an altar
to Jehovah who had appeared to him. And he...
pitched his tent, with Bethel on the west and Ai on
the east; and there he built an altar to Jehovah and
called upon the name of Jehovah.

After Abraham arrived in Canaan,...the first place he went to
was...Shechem, [where] he built an altar. The second place he
went to was Bethel, and there he also built an altar. Later he left
Bethel and went to Egypt. Then he went from Egypt to the south,
and from the south he went back to Bethel, staying in between
Bethel and...Ai....Later he went to another place, Hebron, and
built another altar. In these three places, Abraham built three
altars....The Bible shows us that God used these three places—
Shechem, Bethel, and Hebron—to represent Canaan. (*CWWN,*
vol. 35, "The God of Abraham, Isaac, and Jacob," pp. 30-31)

Today's Reading

The meaning of the word *Shechem* in the original language is
"shoulder." In the human body the shoulder is the place with the
most strength....Therefore *Shechem* can also mean "strength."
The first characteristic of Canaan is strength. This means that
God's strength is in Canaan....The name *Moreh* means "teacher"
or "teaching" in the original language. It has something to do with
knowledge. The oak of Moreh was in Shechem. This means that
knowledge comes from power and that knowledge is the result
of power. In other words, genuine spiritual knowledge comes
from the power of Christ. If we do not have the satisfying power
of the life of Christ, we will not have genuine spiritual knowledge and will not be able to convey anything spiritual to others.

God brought Abraham not only to Shechem, but to Bethel
as well [Gen. 12:8]. The name *Bethel* in the original language
means "the house of God." God is not after hundreds and thousands of strong, but uncoordinated, men like Samson, and He is

not after a pile of unorganized, living stones. God's intention is to build a temple—the house of God. One characteristic of Canaan is that God's people are the temple of God and the house of God.

It is not enough to have Shechem (power) only. There must also be Bethel. All the powerful ones must become God's house and the Body of Christ before they can become useful.

The problem is that many Christians consider the Body of Christ merely as a principle; they have not seen the life of the Body of Christ. What good is it if we try to do something according to a principle without having the life to do it? We think that we should cooperate with one another in everything, and we often reluctantly agree to cooperate, but our heart has no taste for it.... If we do not know that the Body is a life, and if we merely act according to a principle, we are only imitating in an outward way.

The basic condition for knowing the life of the Body is that our tent must be pitched between Bethel and Ai....It is not merely a matter of Bethel, but a matter of Ai as well. The name *Ai* means "a heap."...Bethel is a house, the house of God, while Ai is a heap, a desolate heap,...[which] signifies the old creation; Ai symbolizes the old creation. If we are to turn our face towards God's house, we must turn our back towards the desolate heap. In other words, unless a Christian is dealt with in his fleshly life, he cannot possibly know the Body of Christ. Only when we have Ai on the east will we have Bethel on the west. If we do not have Ai on our east, we will not have Bethel on our west. One begins his experience of the Body of Christ and enjoys and lives out the Body life by dealing with the life of the flesh. If we want to find out what the house of God is, we must deny the desolate heap on the negative side. Only after our natural life has been dealt with by God, and only after we have been subdued to realize that the natural life should be judged rather than praised, will we be joined spontaneously to the other brothers and sisters. Only then will we be able to live out the life of the Body of Christ. (*CWWN,* vol. 35, pp. 31-34)

Further Reading: CWWN, vol. 35, ch. 3

Enlightenment and inspiration: _____

_____

_____

_____

Morning Nourishment

Gen. And Abram moved his tent and came and dwelt by
13:18 the oaks of Mamre, which are in Hebron, and there
he built an altar to Jehovah.
Rev. And I saw the holy city, New Jerusalem, coming
21:2-3 down out of heaven from God....Behold, the taber-
nacle of God is with men, and He will tabernacle
with them...

The name *Hebron* means "fellowship."...God's house is a matter
of life, while fellowship is a matter of living. It is impossible for one
to live in Hebron without first passing through Bethel....Where
there is God's house, there is fellowship. Fellowship is not a com-
munity organized by a number of people. Fellowship can only be
found in the house of God. Without God's house it is impossible to
have fellowship. If our natural life is not dealt with, we cannot
have any fellowship. We live in the Body and have fellowship only
when the natural life is dealt with. (*CWWN*, vol. 35, p. 35)

Today's Reading

The Body is a fact; it is a real, definite fact. In this Body we spontaneously communicate and fellowship with other children of the
Lord. Once we turn our back towards Ai and judge the natural life,
we will enter into the life of the Body of Christ and be brought into
the fellowship spontaneously. Those who truly know the Body of
Christ are freed from individualism spontaneously. They do not
trust in themselves, and they realize that they are very weak.
They fellowship with all the children of God. God must bring us to
the point where we cannot go on without fellowship. God will
show us that what is impossible with individuals is possible when
it is done in fellowship. This is the meaning of Hebron.

In Hebron there were...the oaks of Mamre (Gen. 13:18). The
name *Mamre* means "fatness" or "strength" in the original language. The result of fellowship is fatness and strength. All fatness, riches, and strength come from fellowship.

If our natural life has been dealt with, and if we know what
the life of the Body means, we will learn to treasure the other

brothers and to touch life and receive help in the meetings.... Even the weakest brother or sister can render...some help. (*CWWN,* vol. 35, *"The God of Abraham, Isaac, and Jacob,"* pp. 35-37)

At Hebron Abraham's tent became a place where he had fellowship with God. By Abraham's pitching a tent at Hebron, God had a place on earth where He could communicate and fellowship with man (cf. Gen. 18). Abraham's tent with the altar built by him was a prefigure of the tabernacle with the altar built by the children of Israel after the exodus from Egypt (Exo. 40). That tabernacle was God's testimony (Exo. 38:21) and the place where God and His people could dwell and fellowship together. The ultimate consummation of the tabernacle will be the New Jerusalem, the testimony, the expression, of God in eternity and the eternal dwelling place of God and all His called ones (Rev. 21:2-3 and footnote 1 on verse 3; 21:22 and footnote 2). (Gen. 13:18, footnote 1)

The altar has its issue in the tent [Gen. 12:8]....From then on, Abraham lived in God's house—Bethel....Actually, he lived in a tent before, but God did not mention it. Not until he had built the altar does the Word of God bring the tent into view.

A tent is something movable; it does not take root anywhere. Through the altar God deals with us; through the tent God deals with our possessions....What was not consumed on the altar could only be kept in the tent. Here we see a principle....God leaves some of the things offered on the altar for our own use....We must apply the principle of the tent to all the physical things that He permits us to retain, because they have been given back to us to meet our need in the world. If we do not need them, we should dispose of them. We may use them, but we must not be touched by them....May we learn this lesson. We dare not use anything that has not been placed on the altar, we may not take anything back from the altar, and what God gives back must be kept according to the principle of the tent. (*CWWN,* vol. 37, "The Life of the Altar and the Tent," pp. 92-93)

Further Reading: Life-study of Genesis, msg. 41

Enlightenment and inspiration: _____

_____
_____
_____

Hymns, #974

1   He looked for a city and lived in a tent,
     A pilgrim to glory right onward he went;
     God's promise his solace, so royal his birth,
     No wonder he sought not the glories of earth.

       City! O city fair!
       God's dwelling with man to eternity is there.

2   He looked for a city, his God should prepare;
     No mansion on earth, could he covet or share,
     For had not God told him, that royal abode
     Awaited His pilgrims on ending the road.

3   He looked for a city; if sometimes he sighed
     To be trudging the road, all earth's glory denied,
     The thought of that city changed sighing to song,
     For the road might be rough, but it could not be long.

4   He looked for a city, his goal, Lord, we share
     And know that bright city, which Thou dost prepare
     Is ever our portion, since willing to be
     Just pilgrims with Jesus, our roof a tent tree.

Composition for prophecy with main point and sub-points: _____

_____

_____

_____

_____

_____

_____

_____

_____

_____

_____

_____

_____

_____

_____

_____

_____

_____

_____

_____

_____

_____

_____

_____

_____

_____

_____

_____

_____

_____

_____

_____

_____

_____

_____

_____

The Seed for the Fulfillment of God's Purpose

Scripture Reading: Gen. 12:7; 13:15-16; 15:2-6; Gal. 3:7, 16, 29; Rom. 3:24; 4:2-5

Day 1

I. **For the fulfillment of His purpose God must have the seed (Gen. 12:7; 13:15-16; 15:3, 5):**

A. The seed is first the individual Christ and then the corporate Christ, composed of Christ as the Head and all the believers as the Body (Gal. 3:16, 29; 1 Cor. 12:12).

B. As the seed of Abraham, Christ became the all-inclusive life-giving Spirit so that the believers in Christ, who are Abraham's seed, may inherit the consummated Spirit, the consummation of the processed Triune God, as their divine inheritance—their divine blessing for eternity (15:45b; 2 Cor. 3:17; Gal. 3:14, 29; Acts 26:18; Eph. 1:14a).

C. Christ is the unique seed of Abraham; in God's eyes, Abraham has only one seed, that is, Christ (Gen. 12:7a; 13:15; 21:12; 22:17; Gal. 3:16b):

1. Christ is the seed, and the seed is the heir who inherits the promises (v. 16).

2. Christ is not only the seed who inherits the promises but also the blessing of the promises to be inherited by us.

D. As the seed of Abraham, Christ in His humanity was crucified and became a curse on our behalf, being forsaken by God, so that we might receive the promise of the Spirit as the greatest blessing (vv. 13-14).

Day 2

E. As the seed of Abraham, Christ became not only our Redeemer and Savior but also the life-giving Spirit; the life-giving Spirit—the Spirit as the consummation of the processed Triune God—is a transfigured descendant of Abraham (v. 16; 1 Cor. 15:45b).

F. In order to be the seed of Abraham, we must be in Christ and be one with Christ (Gal. 3:29):

1. Since Abraham has only one seed—Christ—to be Abraham's seed we must be of Christ, be a part of Christ.

2. Because we are one with Christ, the unique seed, we too are Abraham's seed.

G. On the one hand, the seed is the One who fulfills the promise; on the other hand, the seed is those who enjoy the promise, which has been fulfilled (vv. 16, 29):

1. In the matter of fulfilling the promise, we have no part; only Christ, the unique seed, is qualified to fulfill God's promise to Abraham.

2. In the matter of enjoying the fulfilled promise, the seed becomes many—the many sons of Abraham (v. 7):

Day 3

a. In order to enjoy the fulfilled promise, we must be one with Christ (1 Cor. 6:17).

b. Outside of Christ, we cannot enjoy the fulfillment of the promise given by God to Abraham.

c. For fulfillment, the seed is one; for enjoyment, the seed includes all those who believe in Christ (John 3:15-16).

II. **Through faith in Christ Jesus, the unique seed, we are all sons of God and sons of Abraham (Gal. 3:7, 26, 29):**

A. Faith in Christ makes the New Testament believers sons of God, a relationship altogether in life (4:7; Rom. 8:14; Heb. 2:10):

1. Faith in Christ brings us into Christ, making us one with Christ, in whom is the sonship (John 3:15-16).

2. We must be identified with Christ through faith so that in Him we may be sons of God.

3. When we believed into Christ, the divine life with the divine nature—in fact, the Divine Being of the Triune God Himself—entered

into us, and we were born of God to become
sons of God (vv. 15-16, 6; 1 John 3:1).

B. Our true status is that in Christ and by the
organic union we are both sons of God and sons of
Abraham (Gal. 3:26, 7):
   1. Christ is the sphere in which this takes place
      (1 Cor. 1:30; John 15:4-5).
   2. We and Christ have been joined in a marvel-
      ous organic union; because of this union, we
      are sons of God and sons of Abraham (1 Cor.
      6:17).

III. **"The word of Jehovah came to him, saying,…
[He] who will come out from your own body
shall be your heir. And He brought him outside and said, Look now toward the heavens,
and count the stars, if you are able to count
them. And He said to him, So shall your seed
be" (Gen. 15:4-5):**
   A. The seed needed for the fulfillment of God's pur-
      pose could not be anything that Abraham al-
      ready possessed (Eliezer—v. 2) or could produce
      out of himself (Ishmael—16:15).
   B. Only that which God worked into Abraham could
      bring forth from Abraham the required seed.
   C. Likewise, only what God works into us through
      His grace can bring forth Christ as the seed to
      fulfill God's purpose (Gal. 1:16; 2:20; 4:19; Eph.
      3:17; Phil. 2:13).
   D. In order to fulfill God's purpose, we need to
      receive God's grace so that Christ can be wrought
      into us as the seed (John 1:16; 1 Cor. 15:10).

IV. **Abraham "believed Jehovah, and He accounted it to him as righteousness" (Gen. 15:6;
cf. Gal. 3:6; Rom. 4:2-3):**
   A. Believing God was Abraham's spontaneous reac-
      tion to God's repeated appearing to him; his be-
      lieving was the springing up within him of the
      element that God had transfused into him (Acts
      7:2; Gen. 12:1-3; 13:14-17).

B. In Genesis 15:6 Abraham did not believe God to obtain outward blessings for his own existence; he believed that God was able to work something into him to bring forth a seed out of his own being for the fulfillment of God's purpose:
   1. This kind of faith is precious to God and is accounted by Him as righteousness (Rom. 4:3).
   2. Abraham was justified by such a faith (vv. 2, 5).
C. God's reaction to Abraham's believing was to justify him, that is, to account him as righteous (Gen. 15:6):
   1. Abraham believed God's word in a definite way, and God accounted it to him as righteousness (Rom. 4:2-5).
   2. God's justification is not a reward (wages) for our good works (labor); it is grace freely given to us through Christ's redemption (3:24; 4:4):
      a. Since God's justification is reckoned according to His grace, it is not based on or according to our works (vv. 4-5).
      b. Our works can by no means replace God's grace; God's grace must be absolute (3:24).
   3. For God to justify Abraham means that God was happy with Abraham and that Abraham was in harmony with God.

Day 6   D. Abraham's being justified by God was not related to sin; rather, it was for the gaining of a seed to produce a kingdom that will inherit the world (4:3, 13):
   1. Romans 4 indicates that justification is not merely for us to be delivered out of God's condemnation but even more for God to gain many sons to constitute the Body of Christ as the kingdom of God for the fulfillment of His purpose (8:29-30; 12:4-5; 14:17).
   2. Justification enables Abraham and all his believing heirs to inherit the world and to exercise the dominion of God on earth (4:13).

3. The purpose of God's justification is to have a reproduction of Christ in millions of saints, who become the members of His Body; the Body then becomes the kingdom of God on earth (12:4-5; 14:17).

Morning Nourishment

Gen. And Jehovah appeared to Abram and said, To your
12:7 seed I will give this land...

Gal. But to Abraham were the promises spoken and to
3:16 his seed. He does not say, And to the seeds, as concerning many, but as concerning one: "And to your
seed," who is Christ.

The seed of Abraham is first the individual Christ and then the corporate Christ (1 Cor. 12:12), composed of Christ as the Head and all His believers (Gal. 3:29) as the Body. All the believers in Christ, as the members of the corporate Christ, are included in this seed as the heirs of God's promised blessing. Eventually, the eternal New Jerusalem, the great, corporate Christ, will be the ultimate consummation of the seed of Abraham (Gen. 22:17; Rev. 21:12-14). (*The Conclusion of the New Testament,* p. 3301)

Today's Reading

Christ as the seed of Abraham has redeemed us out of the curse of the law so that the blessing of Abraham might come to the nations in Him. Christ died a substitutionary death on the cross to deliver us from the curse brought in by Adam. Then in resurrection Christ, who was the unique seed of Abraham as the last Adam, became the life-giving Spirit. The resurrected Christ as the life-giving Spirit is the transfigured descendant of Abraham, the seed of Abraham, dispensed into us to make us the sons of Abraham, the corporate seed of Abraham, those who can receive and inherit the consummated Spirit as the blessing of Abraham (Gal. 3:7, 14; 4:28). The blessing promised to Abraham comes to us through Christ's redemption; now in Christ all the nations will be blessed. The curse has been taken away, and the blessing has come. Before we believed into Christ and were saved, we were cursed under the law. Having believed into Christ, we are no longer cursed; we are blessed through Christ in His humanity as the seed of Abraham, and we are blessed with the consummated Spirit, who is the consummation of the processed Triune God (3:13-14). As the seed of Abraham, Christ brought to us the processed and consummated Triune God as our blessing for our enjoyment. The all-inclusive Spirit, who the all-inclusive Christ as the seed of Abraham has become, is the aggregate of the all-embracing blessing of the full gospel of God in Christ for the divine dispensing according to the divine economy. (*The Conclusion of the New Testament*, pp. 3294-3295)

We know from Galatians 3:16 that Christ is Abraham's unique seed. Christ is the seed, and the seed is the heir who inherits the promises....In order to inherit the promised blessing, we must be one with Christ. Outside of Him, we cannot inherit the promises given by God to Abraham. In God's eyes Abraham has only one seed, Christ. We must be in Him that we may participate in the promise given to Abraham. He is not only the seed inheriting the promise, but also the blessing of the promise for inheritance. For the Galatian believers to turn back from Christ to the law meant that they would forfeit both the Heir and the inheritance of the promises. (*Life-study of Galatians*, p. 172)

As the seed of Abraham, Christ in His humanity was crucified and became a curse on our behalf to redeem us out of the curse of the law. Galatians 3:1 mentions that Jesus Christ was crucified. Verse 13 goes on to say, "Christ has redeemed us out of the curse of the law, having become a curse on our behalf; because it is written, 'Cursed is everyone hanging on a tree.'" Christ as our Substitute on the cross not only bore the curse for us but also became a curse for us.

Not only did Christ redeem us out from the curse; He even became a curse on our behalf. This indicates that He was absolutely abandoned by God. God forsook Christ economically and also considered Him a curse. On the cross Christ accomplished the great work of bringing us out from the curse of the law, working to bear our sins and to remove the curse. (*The Conclusion of the New Testament*, pp. 3286-3287)

Further Reading: The Conclusion of the New Testament, msgs. 327-328

Enlightenment and inspiration: _____

_____

_____

_____

Morning Nourishment

Gal.   **Christ has redeemed us out of the curse of the law,**
3:13-14 **having become a curse on our behalf; because it is**
written, "Cursed is everyone hanging on a tree"; in
order that the blessing of Abraham might come to
the Gentiles in Christ Jesus, that we might receive
the promise of the Spirit through faith.

The Spirit as the consummation of the Triune God for the
dispensing of Himself into the believers of Christ is the seed of
Abraham (1 Cor. 15:45b; 2 Cor. 3:17-18; Rom. 8:9). The last Adam
mentioned in 1 Corinthians 15:45 is the seed of Abraham. This
seed became not only our Redeemer and Savior but also the life-
giving Spirit. The life-giving Spirit is a transfigured descendant
of Abraham. The top blessing, the consummate blessing, to us
sinners is God Himself as the life-giving Spirit. On the one hand,
the life-giving Spirit is a transfigured descendant of Abraham,
and on the other hand, He is the very Triune God. This life-
giving Spirit is the consummated Spirit who is the consummation of the processed Triune God. This is the real blessing. (*The
Central Line of the Divine Revelation,* pp. 87-88)

Today's Reading

Now, as believers we are no longer merely descendants of
Americans, Chinese, or Japanese. We are Abraham's seed. We
are all one family, and our surname is Abraham, because Abraham is our father (Rom. 4:12).

Our spiritual blessing for eternity is to inherit the consummated Spirit, the consummation of the processed Triune God, as
our inheritance. In the new heaven and new earth in the New
Jerusalem, we will enjoy the processed Triune God, who is the
all-inclusive, consummated, life-giving Spirit. This is our blessing. Even today, the most enjoyable thing to us is the indwelling
Spirit. (*The Central Line of the Divine Revelation,* p. 89)

In Galatians 3:29 Paul continues, "And if you are of Christ,
then you are Abraham's seed, heirs according to promise." Abraham has only one seed, Christ (v. 16). Hence, to be Abraham's seed

we must be of Christ, be a part of Christ. Because we are one with Christ, we too are Abraham's seed, heirs according to promise, inheriting God's promised blessing, which is the all-inclusive Spirit as the ultimate consummation of the processed God, who is our portion. Under the new testament the believers as God's chosen people, being sons of full age, are such heirs, not under law but in Christ. (*The Conclusion of the New Testament,* p. 3300)

In Galatians 3 Paul speaks of the seed of Abraham (vv. 16, 19, 29) and the sons of Abraham (v. 7). The seed is singular, whereas the sons are plural....Concerning God's promise to Abraham, there is the aspect of fulfillment and the aspect of enjoyment. To fulfill the promise is one thing, but to enjoy the blessing of the promise is another. Concerning promises made by one person to another, the one who fulfills the promise is seldom the one who enjoys the blessing of the promise. Usually the person who makes the promise is the one to fulfill the promise, and the one to whom the promise is made is the one who enjoys its blessing. In the case of God's promise to Abraham, God, strictly speaking, is not the one to fulfill the promise. Instead, the promise is fulfilled by the seed, Christ (v. 16). Christ has fulfilled God's promise to Abraham. Thus, the fulfillment of this promise does not depend on the many sons of Abraham, but on the unique seed of Abraham. However, with respect to the enjoyment of the blessing of this promise, the many sons are involved. Whereas the unique seed is the fulfiller, the many sons are the enjoyers.

As the unique seed in Galatians 3, Christ not only inherits the promise, but He also fulfills the promise. The promise God made to Abraham was fulfilled by Christ as Abraham's seed.

In the matter of fulfilling the promise, we have no part. Only Christ, the unique seed, is qualified to fulfill God's promise to Abraham. In this sense, the seed is uniquely one. But in the aspect of enjoying the fulfilled promise, the seed becomes many, the many sons of Abraham. (*Life-study of Galatians,* pp. 171-172)

Further Reading: The Central Line of the Divine Revelation, msgs. 8-9

Enlightenment and inspiration: _____
_____
_____
_____

Morning Nourishment

Gal. Know then that they who are of faith, these are
3:7 sons of Abraham.

26 For you are all sons of God through faith in Christ
Jesus.

29 And if you are of Christ, then you are Abraham's
seed, heirs according to promise.

God intended to give the promise to Abraham according to His eternal purpose. Before this promise was accomplished, the law was given to serve as the custodian of God's chosen people. Then, at the appointed time, Christ, the promised seed, came to fulfill God's promise to Abraham. When Christ came, the fulfillment of God's promised blessing also came. This is grace. Hence, grace came with Christ and with the fulfillment. (*Life-study of Galatians*, p. 178)

Today's Reading

We must turn from the law, the custodian, and stay with Christ, the One who has fulfilled the promise. Of course, this means we should also stay with grace and faith. Then we shall be included in Christ, the unique seed, to inherit the fulfilled promise and to enjoy the blessing of the promise to Abraham. This blessing is the processed Triune God as the all-inclusive life-giving Spirit.

As the unique seed of Abraham, Christ includes all the believers who have been baptized into Him (Gal. 3:27-28). In one sense, when Christ died on the cross, He was crucified alone as our Redeemer. But in another sense, when He was crucified, we were with Him. For the accomplishment of redemption, Christ was crucified alone. But for terminating the old creation, Christ included us in His crucifixion. In the same principle, in the fulfillment of the promise made by God to Abraham, we are not included as part of the unique seed. We can have no share in the fulfillment of this promise. However, for inheriting the promise and enjoying it, we are included. Christ alone fulfilled the promise. But Christ and we share in the enjoyment of the promise. Therefore, on the one hand, the seed is uniquely one; on the other hand, it is all-inclusive. For fulfillment, the seed is one; for inheritance and enjoyment, the seed is all-inclusive, including all believers who have been baptized into Christ.

Works of law make people disciples of Moses (John 9:28) with nothing whatever related to life. Faith in Christ makes the New Testament believers sons of God, a relationship altogether in life. We, the New Testament believers, were born sons of fallen Adam, and in Adam, because of transgressions, we were under the law of Moses. But we have been reborn to become sons of Abraham and have been freed from the law of Moses by faith in Christ. We are sons of Abraham not by natural birth, but by faith. Hence, our being sons of Abraham is based upon the principle of faith. It is based on our believing, not on our working. Our basis for being sons of Abraham surely is not natural descent. We are Abraham's sons according to the principle of faith.

We are both sons of Abraham and sons of God because we have been baptized into Christ and have put on Christ (Gal. 3:27). To believe is to believe into Christ (John 3:16), and to be baptized is to be baptized also into Christ. Faith in Christ brings us into Christ and makes us one with Christ, in whom is the sonship. We must be identified with Christ through faith so that in Him we may be sons of God. By both faith and baptism, we have been immersed into Christ, we have thus put on Christ, and we have become identified with Him.

Some Christians oppose the use of the term *God-men* and even defame us for saying that the believers in Christ, the sons of God through faith in Christ, are God-men. But according to the Bible, it is a divine fact that human beings can become sons of God. When we believed in Christ, the divine life with the divine nature—in fact, the Divine Being of the Triune God Himself—entered into us, and we were born of God to become sons of God. Just as a man's son partakes of his life and nature, so we as God's sons partake of the divine life and nature. (*Life-study of Galatians,* pp. 178, 173-174, 176, 175)

Further Reading: Life-study of Galatians, msgs. 17-19

Enlightenment and inspiration: _____

_____

_____

_____

Morning Nourishment

Gen. But then the word of Jehovah came to him, saying,
15:4-5 This man shall not be your heir, but he who will come
out from your own body shall be your heir. And He
brought him outside and said, Look now toward the
heavens, and count the stars, if you are able to count
them. And He said to him, So shall your seed be.

In what way are the sons of God also the sons of Abraham?
Christ is both the Son of God and the son of Abraham. Because
we are now in Christ, we are sons of God on the one hand and
sons of Abraham on the other hand. How can we be sons of God?
Because we are in Christ, who is the Son of God. How can we be
sons of Abraham? Also because we are in Christ, who is the son
of Abraham. (*Life-study of Galatians,* p. 176)

Today's Reading

It is a matter of tremendous significance for the divine life to
be imparted into us. This impartation of the divine life causes an
organic union which makes us both the sons of God and the sons
of Abraham. This organic union takes place exclusively in
Christ. In Christ we enjoy the wonderful organic union with the
Triune God. In this union we are, on the one hand, the sons of
God and, on the other hand, the sons of Abraham. Christ is the
unique sphere in which this all takes place. When we enter into
this sphere, we become sons of God and sons of Abraham. Our
true status is that in Christ and by the organic union we are
both sons of God and sons of Abraham.

Although we all have a natural life with a natural ancestry, we
need not live any longer according to that life. Instead, we may
live by the divine life with the divine nature. By living according
to this life, we are in reality the sons of God and the sons of Abraham. We have been baptized into Christ, the unique seed who has
fulfilled God's promise to Abraham. We and Christ have been
joined in a marvelous organic union. Because of this union, we are
sons of God and sons of Abraham. Here in this organic union we
inherit the promise which has been fulfilled by Christ. Actually,

Christ Himself is this inheritance. The promise we inherit is the promise we now enjoy. (*Life-study of Galatians,* pp. 176-177)

The seed needed for the fulfillment of God's purpose could not be anything Abraham already possessed (Eliezer—Gen. 15:2) or could produce out of himself (Ishmael—16:15). Only that which God worked into Abraham could bring forth from Abraham the required seed. Likewise, only what God works into us through His grace can bring forth Christ as the seed to fulfill God's purpose. (Gen. 15:4, footnote 1)

The seed that was needed for the fulfillment of God's purpose had to be what God promised to work out through Abraham. It had to be something that God worked into him so that he might bring it forth (Gen. 15:4-5)....If you pray and read Genesis 15 and Galatians 3, you will see that the seed is Christ Himself.

In order to fulfill God's purpose we must have Christ wrought into us. This is why Paul told us that Christ was revealed into him (Gal. 1:15-16), that Christ lived in him (Gal. 2:20), that Christ was formed in him (Gal. 4:19), and that for him to live was Christ (Phil. 1:21). Paul lived Christ. When he was Saul of Tarsus, he passed through a Jewish Damascus, gaining many things. All that he acquired during that time was just an Eliezer. The Lord told Paul that he had to forget all of those things—they were dung, garbage, dog food—and to cast them aside. None of the things that Paul had could bring forth Christ. Only that which God worked into his being could bring forth Christ. The Lord seemed to tell Paul, "The things that you had from your religious background can never bring forth Christ. Only what I am working into you will bring forth Christ. What I am working into you is My grace." Eventually, Paul could say, "By the grace of God I am what I am; and His grace unto me did not turn out to be in vain, but, on the contrary, I labored more abundantly than all of them, yet not I but the grace of God which is with me" (1 Cor. 15:10). (*Life-study of Genesis,* pp. 596-597)

Further Reading: Life-study of Galatians, msg. 20; *Life-study of Genesis,* msg. 44

Enlightenment and inspiration: _____

_____

_____

_____

Morning Nourishment

Gen. And he believed Jehovah, and He accounted it to
15:6 him as righteousness.
Rom. For if Abraham was justified out of works, he has
4:2-3 something to boast in, but not before God. For what
does the Scripture say? "And Abraham believed God,
and it was accounted to him as righteousness."

Believing God was Abraham's spontaneous reaction to God's
repeated appearing to him. God appeared to Abraham a number
of times (Gen. 12:1-3, 7; 13:14-17; 15:1-7; ch. 18; Acts 7:2), each
time transfusing something of His glory, something of Himself,
into Abraham. Hence, Abraham's believing was actually the
springing up within him of the very element that God had
transfused into him. God's reaction to Abraham's believing was
to justify him, that is, to account him righteous. This account-
ing was not out of works but was based on his believing God.
(Rom. 4:3, footnote 1)

Today's Reading

[In Genesis 15:6] Abraham did not believe God to obtain
outward blessings for his own existence; he believed that God
was able to work something into him to bring forth a seed out of
his own being for the fulfillment of God's purpose. This kind of
faith is precious to God and is accounted by Him as righteousness. Abraham was justified by such a faith (Rom. 4:1-5 and
footnote 1 of v. 1). (Gen. 15:6, footnote 1)

[Genesis 15:6] is the first time the Bible speaks of faith.
Abraham is the father of faith. He believed God's word in a definite way, and God counted it to him for righteousness.

God told Abraham, "He who will come out from your own
body shall be your heir" [v. 4]. This shows us that God's goal is
not achieved through the many people He has gathered, but
through those whom He has begotten. Those who are not
begotten of God do not count; they cannot fulfill God's purpose.
God's eternal purpose is fulfilled through those whom He has
begotten.

God asked Abraham if he could count the stars in heaven and told him that his descendants would be as numerous as the stars. Abraham believed in God, and God counted it to him for righteousness. As we have mentioned previously, God first had to work on one person and gain something in him before He could gain something through many others. In order for God to have many believers, He first had to gain one believer. Abraham believed in God, and God counted it to him for righteousness. (*CWWN*, vol. 35, "The God of Abraham, Isaac, and Jacob," p. 47)

God's justification is not a reward (wages) for our good works (labor); it is grace freely given to us through Christ's redemption. If God's justification were based on our good works, or if it required our good works, then it would be the wages we earn for our good works; that is, it would be something owed to us, not something freely given by God. Since God's justification is reckoned according to His grace, it is no longer out of works; otherwise, grace is no longer grace (Rom. 11:6). Our works can by no means replace God's grace; God's grace must be absolute. (Rom. 4:4, footnote 2)

Through our fellowship, I hope we can realize that in God's eyes and in God's heart, Abraham was a special person.

God…promised Abraham that his heavenly seed in their divine nature would be as many as the stars in heaven who could never be touched by anyone on earth. Abraham believed in Jehovah, and Jehovah reckoned this believing to him for righteousness (Gen. 15:5-6). In Romans 4 Paul considered this as the example of justification. God is the shield, God is the great reward, and God is also the Justifier. God's justifying of Abraham meant that God became happy with Abraham and that Abraham was altogether in harmony with God. He was altogether acceptable to God, having no problem with God. (*The History of God in His Union with Man,* pp. 96-97)

Further Reading: CWWN, vol. 35, "The God of Abraham, Isaac, and Jacob," ch. 4; *Life-study of Romans,* msgs. 5-6

Enlightenment and inspiration: _____

_____

_____

_____

Morning Nourishment

Rom. For *it was* not through the law *that* the promise
4:13 *was made* to Abraham or to his seed that he would
be the heir of the world, but through the righteousness of faith.
12:5 So we who are many are one Body in Christ, and
individually members one of another.

There is no mention of sin in Genesis 15. God told Abraham,
"Look at the heavens and count the stars. Your seed will be like
the stars in the sky" [cf. v. 5]. Abraham believed, and his faith
was counted by God as righteousness. God's justification of Abraham was unrelated to sin. It was totally involved with God's purpose, with having a seed to produce a kingdom for the fulfillment of God's purpose. This is why the apostle Paul in Romans 4,
after referring to Genesis 15 where Abraham's faith was reckoned as righteousness, mentions the promise given to Abraham
and his seed of inheriting the world (Rom. 4:13). What does
inheriting the world have to do with justification? Why does
Paul mention this in chapter 4? Abraham and his heirs must
inherit the world for the sake of God's kingdom, and God's kingdom is for His purpose. (*Life-study of Romans*, p. 83)

Today's Reading

Abraham was not justified by faith in Genesis 14 when he
believed that God was the Most High God, the Possessor of
heaven and earth. God did not count that kind of faith to him as
righteousness....It was the faith that believed that God was able
to work something into him to bring forth the seed. Believing that
God will supply our daily needs, our daily food, is good, but it is not
the kind of faith that is precious in the eyes of God. What kind of
faith is precious in God's sight? The faith that believes that He is
able to work Himself into us to bring forth Christ. Most Christians today only care for the faith that believes that God can do
outward things for them. That kind of faith believes that God is
able to give them health, healing, a good job, or a promotion. Many
Christians only have that kind of faith. Although that kind of

faith is good, it is not the faith that is so dear and precious in the eyes of God. He did not count that kind of faith as righteousness to Abraham. The kind of faith that was counted as righteousness to Abraham was the faith that God was able to work something into him to bring forth a seed. In Genesis 15 Abraham did not believe that God would give him bread and butter, cattle, or more servants. He believed that God was able to work something into him and bring forth a seed. (*Life-study of Genesis,* p. 593)

Romans 4 tells us that God's justification is not for going to heaven or merely for our salvation. Justification enables Abraham and all his believing heirs to inherit the world and to exercise the dominion of God on this earth as mentioned in Genesis 1. If we only had Romans 3, we would say that God's justification, based upon Christ's redemption, is for our salvation. Chapter 4, however, clearly unveils that God's justification of His chosen ones is not merely for their salvation; it is purposely for them to inherit the world that they may exercise God's dominion on the earth.

Paul wrote Romans 4 because he wanted to show that God's justification is for the fulfillment of His purpose. God's purpose is to have the one Body, which is the kingdom, to express Him and to exercise His dominion on the earth.

The purpose of God's justification is to have a reproduction of Christ in millions of saints. These saints, as the reproduction of Christ, become the members of His Body (Rom. 12:5). This Body then becomes the kingdom of God on earth (Rom. 14:17) for the fulfillment of God's purpose. The Body as the kingdom of God is expounded in Romans 12—16. All the local churches are expressions of the Body of Christ as the kingdom of God. The church as the kingdom of God is not composed of one Isaac, but of many Isaacs who have proceeded out of God's justification. All of these are the issue of the subjective and deeper experience of justification. (*Life-study of Romans,* pp. 84, 87, 98)

Further Reading: Life-study of Romans, msgs. 7-8

Enlightenment and inspiration: _____

_____

_____

_____

Hymns, #191

1 Lord, Thou art the "Seed of woman,"
     Born to bruise the enemy;
   Thou didst take the human nature,
     Die to win the victory.
   As the very God incarnate,
     Flesh and blood Thou didst partake;
   Thou thru death hast crushed the devil
     And his pow'r of death didst break.

2 "Seed of Abraham," Thou art, Lord,
     By God's promise Thou hast come,
   That the blessing He hath promised
     On all people thus might come.
   Abraham Thou hast preceded,
     For Thou art the great "I AM,"
   Yet Thou cam'st to be his offspring
     And become God's promised "Lamb."

3 Lord, Thou art the "Seed of David,"
     For the kingdom Thou wast raised;
   For God's glory and His building
     On the throne Thou hast been placed.
   Truly Thou art "David's offspring,"
     Yet "my Lord" he calleth Thee,
   For Thou art his "root" and fountain,
     "Lord of all" eternally.

4 Though "a child" born with our nature,
     Thou the "Mighty God" art called;
   Thou, "a son" to us art given,
     "Everlasting Father" called.
   All the blessings God hath promised,
     With our faith on Thee depend;
   Thou art "Yea" and "Amen" for them,
     All the content and the end!

Composition for prophecy with main point and sub-points: _____

_____

_____

_____

_____

_____

_____

_____

_____

_____

_____

_____

_____

_____

_____

_____

_____

_____

_____

_____

_____

_____

_____

_____

_____

_____

_____

_____

_____

_____

_____

_____

_____

The Land for the Fulfillment
of God's Purpose

Scripture Reading: Gen. 12:7; 15:7-21; Gal. 3:14; Col. 1:12; 2:6

Day 1   I. **For the fulfillment of God's purpose two things are required—the seed and the land; both the seed and the land typify Christ, who is the centrality and universality of God's economy (Gen. 12:7; Col. 1:18; 3:10-11).**

II. **The Lord spoke to Abraham repeatedly concerning the land, saying, "Now lift up your eyes, and look from the place where you are, northward and southward and eastward and westward; for all the land that you see I will give to you and to your seed forever...Rise up; walk through the land according to its length and its breadth, for I will give it to you" (Gen. 13:14-15, 17; cf. 12:7; 15:7):**

A. The land was a place for Abraham to live in and live on (vv. 7-8).

B. The land was a place in which Abraham could defeat all his enemies in order that God might have a kingdom on earth (14:13-20).

C. The land was the place where God could have a habitation as the expression of Himself (Deut. 12:5, 11; 16:2).

D. For us today the land is Christ, who is living in us and in whom we are living; we should live in Christ and on Christ (Col. 1:27; 2:6).

Day 2 III. **As typified by the good land, the land of Canaan, Christ is "the allotted portion of the saints" (1:12):**

A. *The allotted portion* refers to the lot of the inheritance, as illustrated by the allotment of the good land of Canaan given to the children of Israel for their inheritance (Josh. 14:1):

1. The New Testament believers' inheritance,

their allotted portion, is the all-inclusive Christ (cf. Deut. 8:7-10).

   2. Christ is the allotted portion of the saints as their divine inheritance for their enjoyment (Eph. 3:8).

  B. Since we have received Christ as our allotted portion, we should walk in Him (Col. 2:6):

    1. To walk is to live, to act, to behave, and to have our being.

    2. We should walk, live, and act in Christ so that we may enjoy His riches, just as the children of Israel lived in the good land, enjoying all its rich produce (Deut. 8:7-10).

    3. The good land today is Christ as the all-inclusive Spirit, who dwells in our spirit to be our enjoyment; to walk according to this Spirit is the central and crucial point of the New Testament (Gal. 3:14; 5:16; 2 Tim. 4:22; Rom. 8:4, 16).

Day 3 **IV. The physical aspect of the blessing that God promised to Abraham was the good land, which is a type of the all-inclusive Christ (Gen. 12:7; 13:15; 17:8; 26:3-4):**

  A. Since Christ is eventually realized as the all-inclusive life-giving Spirit, the blessing of the promised Spirit corresponds with the blessing of the land promised to Abraham (Gal. 3:14; 1 Cor. 15:45; 2 Cor. 3:17).

  B. Actually, the Spirit as the realization of Christ in our experience is the good land as the source of God's bountiful supply for us to enjoy (Gen. 12:7; Deut. 8:7; Gal. 3:14).

Day 4 **V. The land is Christ as the all-inclusive Spirit, and it is also the church, the Body of Christ, as the enlargement, the expansion, of Christ (1 Cor. 12:12-13):**

  A. In the church we live in Christ and on Christ (Col. 2:6; 3:4, 10-11).

B. In the church we defeat the enemies, and we have the kingdom of God with the dwelling place of God (Eph. 6:10-12; 2:22; Rom. 14:17).

C. In order to fulfill God's purpose, we need to receive God's grace so that Christ can be wrought into us as the seed and lived out of us as the land to be our church life, that we may enjoy God's rest, defeat God's enemies, and establish God's kingdom with His dwelling place for His expression and representation (Gen. 1:26; Gal. 6:18; 3:16; 4:19; Col. 1:12; 2:6; Heb. 4:9; Eph. 6:10-12; 2:22; Matt. 6:33).

D. At a certain time, after we have truly become nothing, God will work Himself in Christ into us, and that which He has worked into us will bring forth Christ as the seed and will also bring us into Christ as our land (Eph. 3:17, 8; Col. 1:12, 27; 2:6).

Day 5 **VI. In Genesis 15:7-21 God made a covenant with Abraham concerning the land:**

A. Because Abraham lacked faith to believe God for the promise concerning the land, God confirmed His promise to Abraham concerning the land by making a covenant with him (vv. 8-21).

B. The extraordinary way in which God enacted this covenant implies the way in which Abraham could fulfill God's eternal purpose (vv. 10-18):

1. The covenant God made with Abraham was a covenant of promise that would be fulfilled through God's power in His grace, not through Abraham's effort in his flesh; the new testament is a continuation of this covenant (Gal. 3:17-18).

2. God made His covenant with Abraham through the crucified and resurrected Christ (Gen. 15:9-10):

a. The three kinds of slain cattle signify Christ in His humanity being crucified for us, and the two living birds signify

Christ in His divinity being the living, resurrected One (John 11:25).

b. Christ was killed in His humanity, but He lives in His divinity (14:19; 1 Pet. 3:18).

Day 6
3. God's asking Abraham to offer the cattle and the birds to Him implies that Abraham had to identify himself with and be one with all the things that he offered (Gen. 15:9-10):

a. This indicates that in order to fulfill God's eternal purpose, we must be crucified in Christ's crucifixion and resurrected in Christ's resurrection (Rom. 6:5, 8; Gal. 2:20).

b. Only in this way can we practice the church life in Christ as the promised land (Col. 1:12; 2:6; 3:10-13).

4. In His covenant with Abraham God set the boundaries of the good land, the land of Immanuel, the territory of Israel, from the Nile to the Euphrates; this is the land that Christ, the unique seed of Abraham, will inherit for the establishing of His millennial kingdom (Gen. 15:18; 12:7; Isa. 8:8; Gal. 3:16; cf. Exo. 23:31; Deut. 11:24 and footnote 1; Josh. 1:3-4; Matt. 25:34 and footnote 1).

Morning Nourishment

Gen. And Jehovah appeared to Abram and said, To your
12:7 seed I will give this land...
13:14-15 And Jehovah said to Abram after Lot had separated from him, Now lift up your eyes, and look
from the place where you are, northward and
southward and eastward and westward; for all the
land that you see I will give to you and to your seed
forever.

Both the seed and the land are Christ. The seed is Christ in
us and the land is the Christ in whom we live. Christ lives in us
as the seed, and we live in Him as the land. He is both the seed
and the land for the fulfillment of God's eternal purpose. (*Life-
study of Genesis,* pp. 601-602)

Today's Reading

Many Christians think that the land is heaven, considering
physical death as the Jordan River. This concept is altogether
not according to the proper understanding of the holy Word.
During Abraham's time, the land was a place in which he could
live. Abraham needed a place to live in and to live on. Hence, the
land is a place for God's people to live in and to live on. Furthermore, during Abraham's time, the land was a place in which
Abraham could defeat all of his enemies in order that God
might have a kingdom on earth. Moreover, the land was the
place where God could have a habitation as the expression of
Himself. Thus, we see five points concerning the land: that it
was a place for God's people to live in, a place for them to live on,
a place where God's enemies could be defeated, a place where
God could have His kingdom, and a place where God could have
a habitation for His expression. Eventually, in the land, the
kingdom of God was established, the temple was built for God's
habitation, and the glory of God was manifested. All of that was
a miniature of the fulfillment of God's purpose. This was altogether a different matter from Abraham's existence. It was one
thing for Abraham to exist; it was another thing for him to have

the seed and the land for the fulfillment of God's purpose.

What is the land for us today? Undoubtedly, the land is Christ who is living in us and in whom we are living. Today, we must live in Christ and on Christ. But many Christians do not practice this. They care neither for Christ's being wrought into them as the seed nor for their living in Christ as their land for the fulfillment of God's purpose. To them, Christ is not the land for them to live in and to live on; neither is He the land for them to slaughter all their enemies. Where can we slaughter our enemies? In Christ our land. Christ is the very place in which we slaughter our Chedorlaomer and all of the other kings. Christ is also the land for the kingdom of God where God's habitation can be built.

The land actually symbolizes Christ. In type, the land is the place where God's people have rest and where God can defeat all of His enemies and establish His kingdom with His habitation for His expression and representation. Please remember the following points regarding the land: that it is the place where God's people may have rest; that it is the place where all of God's enemies can be slaughtered; and that it is the place where God establishes His kingdom and builds up His habitation that He may be expressed and represented on this rebellious earth. What is qualified to be such a land? Nothing other than Christ. In Christ, we have rest and we slaughter the enemies. In Christ, God establishes His kingdom and builds His habitation, the church, for His expression and representation. Have you seen that both the seed and the land are Christ? The seed that God promised Abraham is today the corporate Christ, and the land that God promised him is the wonderful resurrected and elevated Christ in whom we rest and slaughter our enemies and in whom God establishes His kingdom and builds up His habitation that He might be expressed and represented. (*Life-study of Genesis,* pp. 599-600, 604)

Further Reading: Life-study of Genesis, msgs. 44-45

Enlightenment and inspiration: _____

_____

_____

_____

Morning Nourishment

Col. Giving thanks to the Father, who has qualified you
1:12 for a share of the allotted portion of the saints in
the light.

2:6 As therefore you have received the Christ, Jesus
the Lord, walk in Him.

Gal. But I say, Walk by the Spirit and you shall by no
5:16 means fulfill the lust of the flesh.

God's promise to Abraham with respect to the good land is of
great significance. When Paul was writing the Epistle to the
Colossians and was speaking of the portion of the saints, he no
doubt had in mind the picture of the allotting of the good land to
the children of Israel in the Old Testament. The Greek word rendered "portion" in 1:12 can be also rendered "lot." Paul used this
term with the Old Testament record of the land as the background. God gave His chosen people, the children of Israel, the
good land for their inheritance and enjoyment. The land meant
everything to them....[Even today] the problem in the Middle
East regarding Israel and the surrounding nations is a problem
of the land. (*Life-study of Colossians,* p. 48)

Today's Reading

As we have received Christ, we should walk in Him. To walk is
to live, to act, to behave, and to have our being. We should walk, live,
and act in Christ so that we may enjoy His riches, just as the children of Israel lived in the good land and enjoyed all its rich produce.

In our experience Christ should be the good land in which we
live and walk. This should not merely be a doctrine to us. We need
to pray, "Lord, I want to live and walk in You. Lord, I pray that You
will be the good land to me in my experience, and that every
aspect of my living may be in You."

[In Galatians 3:14] Paul refers to the blessing of Abraham and
the promise of the Spirit. This blessing refers to the good land,
and the fulfillment of this blessing for us today is Christ as the all-
inclusive Spirit. Therefore, according to Paul's concept, to walk
in Christ as the good land is to walk in the all-inclusive Spirit.

In Colossians 2:6 Paul tells us to walk in Christ, but in Galatians 5:16 he charges us to walk by the Spirit. Furthermore, in Romans 8:4 he speaks of walking according to spirit. These verses indicate that the good land for us today is the all-inclusive Spirit who indwells our spirit. This all-inclusive Spirit is the all-inclusive Christ as the processed Triune God. After being processed, the Triune God is the all-inclusive Christ as the all-inclusive Spirit for us to experience. Today this all-inclusive Spirit indwells our spirit to be our good land.

Christ is the embodiment of God and the expression of God. Through incarnation, He became the last Adam, who was crucified on the cross for our redemption. In resurrection this last Adam became a life-giving Spirit (1 Cor. 15:45). Therefore, in 2 Corinthians 3:17 Paul says, "And the Lord is the Spirit." Because Christ as the life-giving Spirit dwells in our spirit, we are one spirit with Him. In 2 Timothy 4:22 Paul says, "The Lord be with your spirit," and in 1 Corinthians 6:17, "He who is joined to the Lord is one spirit." Therefore, Christ as the all-inclusive good land is now in our spirit. Concerning this, we all need the riches of the full assurance of understanding.

Having the full assurance that the all-inclusive Spirit is mingled with our spirit, we should set our minds on this mingled spirit (Rom. 8:6). By doing this, we are spontaneously setting our minds on Christ. Then we must go on to walk in this mingled spirit. This means that we must live, move, behave, and have our being according to the spirit. In this way we shall experience Christ and enjoy Him as the good land. Nothing in the New Testament is more central, crucial, and vital than walking according to the mingled spirit. Christ as the all-inclusive Spirit dwells in our spirit to be our life, our person, and our everything. Our need today is to return to Him, to set our minds on the spirit, and to walk according to the spirit. This is to walk in Christ as the mystery of God. (*Life-study of Colossians,* pp. 159, 167-168)

Further Reading: Life-study of Colossians, msgs. 6, 19-20

Enlightenment and inspiration: _____

_____

_____

_____

Morning Nourishment

Gal. **In order that the blessing of Abraham might come**
3:14 **to the Gentiles in Christ Jesus, that we might re-**
    ceive the promise of the Spirit through faith.
1 Cor. **...The last Adam** *became* **a life-giving Spirit.**
15:45

Because it combines the promise of the Spirit with the blessing of Abraham, Galatians 3:14 is extremely important. The
blessing of Abraham is the blessing promised by God to Abraham (Gen. 12:3) for all the nations of the earth. This promise was
fulfilled, and this blessing has come to the nations in Christ
through His redemption by the cross. The context of Galatians
3:14 indicates that the Spirit is the blessing which God promised
to Abraham for all the nations and which has been received by
the believers through faith in Christ. The Spirit is the compound
Spirit and actually is God Himself processed in His trinity
through incarnation, crucifixion, resurrection, ascension, and
descension for us to receive as our life and our everything. This is
the focus of the gospel of God.

The physical aspect of the blessing God promised to Abraham was the good land (Gen. 12:7; 13:15; 17:8; 26:3-4), which was
a type of the all-inclusive Christ (Col. 1:12). Since Christ is eventually realized as the all-inclusive life-giving Spirit (1 Cor. 15:45;
2 Cor. 3:17), the blessing of the promised Spirit corresponds to
the blessing of the promised land. Actually, the Spirit as the realization of Christ in our experience is the good land as the source
of God's bountiful supply for us to enjoy. (*Life-study of Galatians,*
pp. 130-131)

Today's Reading

Galatians 3:14 does not say that in receiving the blessing of
Abraham we receive Christ. Instead, this verse tells us that we receive the Spirit. Surely this indicates that the Spirit here is
the blessing of Abraham....What Spirit would be the all-inclusive
blessing, which is Christ as the seed and as the land? It must be
the Spirit, the all-inclusive life-giving Spirit. First Corinthians
15:45 says that the last Adam became a life-giving Spirit, and

2 Corinthians 3:17 declares that now the Lord is the Spirit.

At the time of the Lord's incarnation, the Holy Spirit began to have the element of humanity as well as divinity. From that time, the Holy Spirit was compounded with the Lord's human living, crucifixion, and resurrection and became the Spirit, the all-inclusive Spirit compounded with divinity, humanity, and the Lord's human living, death, and resurrection. All that God has purposed and planned and all that He has accomplished through incarnation, human living, crucifixion, and resurrection are included in *the* Spirit. Hence, *the* Spirit is all-inclusive, the Triune God processed to be everything to us. This Spirit is the blessing of the gospel.

The Spirit we have received as the blessing of the gospel is the all-inclusive, compound Spirit typified by the compound ointment in Exodus 30:23-25. The compounding of the spices with the olive oil to produce the ointment typifies the compounding of Christ's humanity, death, and resurrection with the Spirit of God to produce the all-inclusive Spirit. This Spirit is the bountiful supply to the believers in God's New Testament economy (Gal. 3:5; Phil. 1:19). By faith we have received this Spirit as the blessing of the gospel promised to Abraham by God. As the processed Triune God, the Spirit is the full realization of the all-inclusive Christ as the good land.

Since the Spirit in Galatians denotes the processed Triune God, we may say that the good land is the very processed Triune God. In the gospel what God gives us is nothing less than Himself.

We can say that the processed Triune God is the all-inclusive One who is everything to us and that this One is our good land. When the children of Israel entered into the good land, they had no lack. Therefore, this good land is a type of the processed Triune God who is realized in full as the all-inclusive Spirit indwelling our spirit. The good land today is in our spirit. (*Life-study of Galatians,* pp. 131-132, 134, 149-150)

Further Reading: Life-study of Galatians, msgs. 15, 17

Enlightenment and inspiration: _____

_____

_____
_____

Morning Nourishment

1 Cor. 12:12-13 **For even as the body is one and has many members, yet all the members of the body, being many, are one body, so also is the Christ. For also in one Spirit we were all baptized into one Body, whether Jews or Greeks, whether slaves or free, and were all given to drink one Spirit.**

Eph. 2:22 **In whom you also are being built together into a dwelling place of God in spirit.**

In this matter of God's purpose we should not count on what we have or on what we can do. What we have is Eliezer and what we can do is Ishmael. Eliezer was what Abraham had and Ishmael was what Abraham could do, and neither of them counted for the fulfillment of God's purpose. What we have and what we can do does not count. It has to be God Himself. After a certain time, when we truly have become nothing, God will work Himself into us, and that which He has worked into us will bring forth Christ as the seed and will also bring us into Christ as our land. Christ should be the seed within us. Christ should also be the land in which we live. (*Life-study of Genesis,* p. 601)

Today's Reading

The Body of Christ, the church, is the expansion of Christ. In the church we live in Christ and on Christ; in the church we slaughter the enemies; and in the church we have the kingdom of God with the habitation of God. For this reason, when we came into the church, we immediately had the sensation that we had come home. Now we are no longer wandering but have a place in which and on which to live, a place in which to slaughter all our enemies, a place in which we may have the kingdom of God with the habitation of God. Before we came into the church, we did not have the proper Christian living, but after coming into the church, what a positive change has happened to our living! Before coming into the church, it was difficult for us to defeat any of our enemies, but after coming into the church, it was so easy. Chedorlaomer is afraid of the church. Where can we slaughter all of our enemies? In Canaan. What is today's Canaan? It is the church, the enlarged Christ. Where is the kingdom of God with God's habitation today? Also in the church. The church, the enlarged Christ, is our good land today.

To believe that Christ is the seed is easy, but to believe that Christ is the land is difficult. It is easier to believe that Christ is our life than it is to believe that Christ can be our church life. Many Christians believe in God for Christ's being their life, but when they come to the matter of the church life, the good land where we can rest, slaughter the enemies, and afford God the ground to establish His kingdom and build up His habitation, they say that it is impossible for us to have this today. Many Christians seem to be saying, "It is possible for us to live by Christ, but it is impossible to have the church life." It is easier for them to believe that Christ can be their life than that the church can be their living....Once again we see that we are the same as Abraham, finding it easy to believe in God for the seed but finding it difficult to believe in Him for the land. Do you have Christ as the seed? Do you also have Him as the land? It is not such a simple matter to have Christ as the land for us to live in so that we may have the church life and that God may have His kingdom with His habitation for His expression and representation.

Years ago, before we came into the church life, we ministered on the matter of living by Christ, but we ourselves were not in the rest. We wandered restlessly until one day, by His grace, we came into the church. When we came into the church, we began to have the sensation that we were in the rest. Before we came into the church life, it was very difficult for us to slaughter the enemies, but after coming into the church life, we found that it was easy to slaughter them all. In the church life God's kingdom is set up, His habitation is built up, and God is expressed and represented. This is the fulfillment of God's eternal purpose today. (*Life-study of Genesis,* pp. 601, 605)

Further Reading: Life-study of Genesis, msgs. 44-45

Enlightenment and inspiration: _____

_____

_____

_____

Morning Nourishment

Gen. And He said to him, Bring Me a three-year-old heifer
15:9 and a three-year-old female goat and a three-year-
      old ram and a turtledove and a young pigeon.
John Jesus said..., I am the resurrection and the life; he
11:25 who believes into Me, even if he should die, shall live.
14:19 Yet a little while and the world beholds Me no
      longer, but you behold Me; because I live, you also
      shall live.

Because Abraham found it difficult to believe in God regarding the promise of the land, God was forced to make a covenant
with him....In making His covenant with Abraham, God told
him to take a heifer, a female goat, a ram, a turtledove, and a
young pigeon (Gen. 15:9). The three cattle, all of which were
three years of age, were divided in half, but the two birds were
not; they were kept alive. It was through these that God made
His covenant with Abraham, implying that it was in this way
that Abraham could fulfill God's eternal purpose.

We need to see the significance of the three cattle and the two
birds. In typology, all things offered to God by man are a type of
Christ. Based upon this principle, each of these five things undoubtedly is a type of Christ. Christ is firstly the crucified Christ,
the cut Christ, and secondly He is the resurrected, living Christ. If
we see this, then we can immediately understand that the three
cattle, which were cut and killed, are types of the crucified
Christ. The crucified Christ was the One who became flesh,
living on earth in His humanity. John 1 says that the Word who
was God became flesh (v. 14). Then it speaks of this One as the
Lamb of God (v. 29). The Lamb of God was the One who was the
Word of God becoming flesh. Thus, the three cattle in Genesis 15
should signify Christ in His humanity being crucified for us.
(*Life-study of Genesis,* pp. 605-607)

Today's Reading

The two birds, neither of which was killed, signify the resurrected, living Christ (Lev. 14:6-7). This resurrected Christ is

mainly in His divinity because, according to the Bible, a dove in typology signifies the Holy Spirit (John 1:32). Therefore, while the cattle typify Christ in His humanity, the birds typify Him in His divinity. So the birds in Genesis 15 signify the heavenly Christ, the Christ who came from and who still is in heaven (John 3:13), the Christ who was and who still is living. Christ has been crucified, yet He lives. He was killed in His humanity, but He lives in His divinity. He was killed as a man who walked on this earth, but now He is living as the heavenly One soaring in the heavens. While His humanity was good for Him to be all the sacrifices, His divinity is good for Him to be the living One. He was sacrificed for us in His humanity, and He is living for us in His divinity.

In typology, the turtledove signifies a suffering life and the young pigeon signifies a believing life, a life of faith. While He was living on earth, the Lord Jesus was always suffering and believing. In His suffering life He was the turtledove and in His believing life He was the young pigeon.

There were two birds, and the number two means testimony, bearing witness (Acts 5:32). The two living birds bear testimony of Christ as the resurrected One living in us and for us (John 14:19-20; Gal. 2:20). The living Jesus is the testimony, the One who constantly bears witness. In Revelation 1 the Lord Jesus said, "I am...the living One, and I became dead, and behold, I am living forever and ever" (vv. 17-18). His living forever is His testimony, for the testimony of Jesus is always related to the matter of being living. If a local church is not living, it does not have the testimony of Jesus. The more living we are, the more we are the testimony of the living Jesus.

There were three cattle and two birds, making a total of five items. The number five is the number of responsibility, indicating here that Christ as the crucified and living One is now bearing all the responsibility for the fulfillment of God's eternal purpose. (*Life-study of Genesis,* pp. 608-609)

Further Reading: Life-study of Genesis, msg. 45

Enlightenment and inspiration: _____

_____

_____

_____

Morning Nourishment

Rom. **Now if we have died with Christ, we believe that**
6:8 **we will also live with Him.**

Gal. **I am crucified with Christ; and** *it is* **no longer I** *who*
2:20 **live, but** *it is* **Christ** *who* **lives in me; and the** *life* **which**
I now live in the flesh I live in faith, the *faith* **of the**
Son of God, who loved me and gave Himself up for me.

In [Genesis 15:18] the Lord made a covenant with Abraham....
Abraham's seed was given a spacious land, from the river of
Egypt to the great river of Euphrates. The nation of Israel today
has only a narrow strip of land, but the promised land is more
spacious than this. In typology, this means that after all of the
experiences of affliction, the church life will be expanded and
become spacious. Then we shall have a richer seed and a wider,
broader church life. The seed within us will be richer, and the
land without us will be broader. It is here that we fulfill God's
eternal purpose. (*Life-study of Genesis,* p. 614)

Today's Reading

Whenever people offered something to God in the Old Testament, they laid their hand upon the sacrifice, signifying their
union or identification with it. [In Genesis 15], God's asking Abraham to offer the cattle and birds to Him implied that Abraham
had to be one with all of the things that he offered to God. God
seemed to be saying to him, "Abraham, you must be in union
with all of the things that you offer to Me. You must be identified
with the cattle and the birds." This indicates that we also have to
be cut in Christ's being cut and crucified in His crucifixion. Our
natural man, our flesh, and our self must be cut and crucified.
As we are identified with Him in His crucifixion, we are also
identified with Him in His resurrection. We are dead in His
death (Rom. 6:5a, 8a) and we are living in His resurrection
(Rom. 6:5b, 8b) to fulfill God's purpose. We were terminated in
His crucifixion and we were germinated in His resurrection. It is
in this way that we are enabled to fulfill God's eternal purpose.

It is impossible for the natural man to have the church life.

Among us we have many different kinds of brothers and sisters. Humanly speaking, it is impossible for us to be one. Nevertheless, in the church we are truly one by the crucified and resurrected Christ. We are so one in Him that even the devil has to admit that we are one. Our old man was terminated in Christ's crucifixion. Whenever my terminated old man comes out of the grave, I immediately rebuke him, saying, "What are you doing here? You have been terminated already. It is wrong for you to come here." We all have been terminated in Christ's crucifixion and germinated in His resurrection. In His resurrection we all are living, not living by ourselves but by the resurrected Christ who lives within us and who enables us to have the church life.

Now we see how God can have such a wonderful seed and land as the people and the sphere in and with which He can establish His kingdom and build up His habitation for His expression and representation. How can God do this? Only by Christ's being crucified as our peace offering, sin offering, and burnt offering and being resurrected to be our life. Now we, the called ones, those who offer Christ to God and are identified with Him, are one with Christ. When Christ was crucified and resurrected, we also were crucified and resurrected with Him....Now we can all declare, "It is no longer I who live, but it is Christ who lives in me" (Gal. 2:20). It is by this fact that we can be living today in order to have the church life. In the church life we have Christ within as the seed and Christ without as the land. How can we get into such a land, into such a church life? Only through the crucified and resurrected Christ, through the heifer, female goat, ram, turtledove, and pigeon. On the one hand, we all have been crucified; on the other hand, we all are living. So here God can have the seed and the land for the fulfillment of His eternal purpose. Hallelujah for such a Christ as the seed for us to live by and as the land for us to live in! (*Life-study of Genesis,* pp. 610-612)

Further Reading: Life-study of Genesis, msg. 45; *Truth Lessons— Level Two,* vol. 1, lsn. 4

Enlightenment and inspiration: _____

_____

_____

_____

Hymns, #1164

1   Jesus, the all-inclusive land,
     Is everything to me:
   A Christ of brooks, of depths and streams,
     And fountains bubbling free.
   Springing from valleys and from hills,
   Flowing till every part He fills,
   He waters us—how glorious—
     By His life!

2   Jesus is now the land of wheat—
     Incarnate, crucified.
   But resurrection life is He
     By barley signified.
   He is a land of figs and vines—
   Blood of the grape, the cheering wine.
   With such supplies He satisfies—
     Christ our land!

3   O what a rich, abundant Christ:
     Our pomegranate true,
   The olive tree whose oil is now
     Anointing us anew.
   Rich milk and honey He doth bring,
   Sweet, satisfying, nourishing.
   Our Christ is such; He is so much!
     What a Christ!

4   In our good land we eat the bread—
     There is no scarcity.
   We never lack one thing in Him,
     So rich, so full is He.
   He is a land so vast, immense;
   He is complete in every sense.
   How He expands—land of all lands—
     In our heart!

5   Christ is a land of iron stones,
     Whence comes authority.
   We must dig out this solid Christ
     To bind His enemy.
   Then we must through the sufferings pass
   To be refined as burnished brass.
   With iron bind, as brass refined,
     Is our need.

6   Lord, how we bless Thee for this land,
      The all-inclusive Christ!
   We've eaten Him, we're filled with Him,
      O how He has sufficed!
   Teach us to labor constantly
   Upon this vast reality;
   This is our joy, this our employ—
      Christ our land!

Composition for prophecy with main point and sub-points: _____

_____

_____

_____

_____

_____

_____

_____

_____

_____

_____

_____

_____

_____

_____

_____

_____

_____

_____

_____

_____

_____

_____

_____

_____

_____

_____

_____

_____

Enjoying Christ in His Heavenly Ministry
by Fighting for the Brother

Scripture Reading: Gen. 14; Heb. 7:1-4, 25-26; 8:2

Day 1   **I. To live by faith, as Abraham did, is to cooperate with Christ in His heavenly ministry, not
only by living a life of the altar and the tent
but also by fighting for the brother (Gen.
12:7-8; ch. 14; Rom. 4:12):**

A. Lot made the mistake of separating himself
from Abraham and moving his tent as far as
Sodom (Gen. 13:5-12); "now the men of Sodom
were very wicked and sinful toward Jehovah"
(v. 13):

1. To leave Abraham was to leave God's goal
and God's protection (cf. Phil. 3:17; 1 Cor.
4:16-17; Heb. 13:7).

2. We need to join ourselves to and follow the
proper persons in God's economy so that we
may be kept in the line of life and the flow of
the Lord's move (1 Cor. 15:33; Prov. 13:20;
2 Tim. 1:15-18; 2:22).

B. Because the land around Sodom was rich, Lot
journeyed toward Sodom; eventually, he moved
into the city, lived there, and settled there; under
God's sovereignty Sodom was conquered, and Lot
was taken captive (Gen. 14:12; cf. Jer. 2:13).

Day 2   C. Abraham did not count the weak point of his
brother and did not take pleasure in Lot's suffering and calamity; as far as Abraham was concerned, it was a shame for him to see that his
brother had been captured (1 John 5:16a; Isa.
58:6-7; Prov. 10:12; James 5:19-20).

D. When Abraham received the information about
Lot's capture, he made a strong decision to fight
for Lot; also, before he went out to war, he
prayed, lifting up his hand to Jehovah, God the

Most High, Possessor of heaven and earth (Gen. 14:14, 22; 1 Tim. 2:8).

E. Abraham decided to take his three hundred eighteen men and fight against the four kings and their armies due to the fact that behind the scene Melchizedek (meaning "king of righteousness"), king of Salem (meaning "peace"), was interceding for Lot, Abraham, and Abraham's fighting (Gen. 14:18-20; Heb. 7:1-4, 25-26; 4:14-16; Rom. 8:26-29, 34).

Day 3 II. **After Abraham's victory "Melchizedek the king of Salem brought out bread and wine. Now he was priest of God the Most High" (Gen. 14:18):**

A. Melchizedek is a type of Christ as the kingly High Priest; after Abraham gained the victory, Melchizedek appeared (Heb. 5:6, 10; 7:1-3).

B. Before his appearing, Melchizedek, a priest of God, must have been interceding for Abraham; it must have been through his intercession that Abraham was able to slaughter the four kings and gain the victory (cf. Exo. 17:8-13).

C. Today Christ, our High Priest, is interceding for us in a hidden way (Rom. 8:34; Heb. 7:25) that we may be His overcomers to defeat God's enemies, so that through our victory Christ can be manifested openly in His second coming (cf. Matt. 26:29):

1. We all need to echo the Lord's intercession; if we turn to our spirit and contact Him, there will always be some echoing (cf. Psa. 27:8).

2. If we go according to that echoing, forgetting our environment, enemies, and even ourselves, we shall gain the victory and "slaughter the kings" (such as the self, the natural mind, the wild emotion, the stubborn will, and other enemies).

3. At the end of our slaughter of all the kings, our Melchizedek will appear to us; that will

be the second coming of Christ; then all the earth will realize that God is the Possessor of heaven and earth.

Day 4

D. The priesthood according to the order of Melchizedek is mentioned in the Scriptures (Gen. 14:18) before the priesthood of Aaron (Exo. 28:1); the priesthood according to the order of Melchizedek is higher than the Aaronic priesthood (Heb. 7):

1. In His earthly ministry Christ was a High Priest according to the order of Aaron for the putting away of sin (9:14, 26).

2. Then, in His heavenly ministry Christ was designated a High Priest according to the order of Melchizedek (5:6, 10) for the overcoming of sin, not to offer sacrifices for sin but to minister to us the very God who was processed through incarnation, human living, crucifixion, and resurrection, signified by the bread and the wine (Matt. 26:26-28), as our life supply that we may be saved to the uttermost (Heb. 7:25).

3. To know Christ as the High Priest in His kingship as the King of righteousness and the King of Salem is to be under His headship and lordship, allowing Him as the life-giving Spirit to rule within us for us to become the New Jerusalem, where both righteousness and peace reign (vv. 1-3; Isa. 9:6; 32:1, 17; 2 Pet. 3:13; Eph. 1:10).

4. To know Christ in His heavenly priesthood is to contact Him so that we may be saturated, soaked, and mingled with Him by entering into His praying for us, His taking care of our case before God, and His ministering to us the processed God as the bread and the wine (Matt. 26:26-28).

III. **The apostolic ministry in cooperation with Christ's heavenly ministry "fights for the** brother" by interceding for the saints according to God and His economy and by ministering the processed God into the saints for their overcoming supply and enjoyment (Heb. 7:25; 8:2; Luke 22:31-32; John 21:15-17; Acts 6:4; Rev. 1:12-13; cf. Exo. 28:9-12, 15-21, 29-30).

Day 5 IV. The way to enjoy Christ in His heavenly ministry as the kingly High Priest (Psa. 110:4) is revealed in Psalm 110:3—"Your people will offer themselves willingly / In the day of Your warfare, / In the splendor of their consecration. / Your young men will be to You / Like the dew from the womb of the dawn":

A. In the eyes of the Lord our willing consecration, our offering ourselves to Him, is a matter of splendor; although the church has become degraded, throughout the centuries there has been a line of those who have offered themselves willingly to the Lord in the splendor, the beauty, of their consecration.

B. The word *splendor* may also be translated "adornment"; the splendor of consecration is an adornment; if we offer ourselves willingly to the Lord, we will be beautified with a divine, heavenly splendor.

C. According to the poetry here, the dew with which Christ is watered comes from "the womb of the dawn":

1. We need to enter into this womb to be conceived as the dew with which to water Christ; this involves our morning watch.

2. If we do not rise up early in the morning to contact the Lord, we will miss the opportunity to enter into the womb of the dawn to be made dew for Christ's watering.

3. May we respond to Him by saying, "Lord Jesus, I want to be the dew conceived and produced by the womb of the dawn for You to be watered."

Day 6 V. **After Abraham's victory Melchizedek "blessed him and said, Blessed be Abram of God the Most High, / Possessor of heaven and earth; / And blessed be God the Most High, / Who has delivered your enemies into your hand. And Abram gave him a tenth of all...Abram said to the king of Sodom, I have lifted up my hand to Jehovah, God the Most High, Possessor of heaven and earth, that I will not take a thread or a sandal thong or anything that is yours, lest you say, I have made Abram rich" (Gen. 14:19-20, 22-23):**

A. Because Abraham, an overcomer, had gained the victory over God's enemies and was standing with God on the earth, God could be referred to not only as the God of heaven (2 Chron. 36:23; Neh. 1:5; 2:4, 20) but also as the Possessor of heaven and earth (Gen. 14:19, 22).

B. Abraham overcame the temptation of earthly substance, displaying his purity in this matter; the manifestation of our enjoyment of Christ in His heavenly ministry is seen in the way we handle our material possessions:

1. For the Lord's move on earth, we need to follow the pattern of Abraham by honoring our ascended Lord with our earthly substance (v. 20; Heb. 7:2, 4; cf. Mal. 3:8-10; Luke 6:38).

2. For the Lord's move on earth, we need to overcome the temptation of earthly substance by enjoying the riches of the processed Triune God (Gen. 14:21-24; cf. 2 Kings 5:15-27; 3 John 7-8).

Morning Nourishment

Gen. **So Lot chose for himself the entire plain of the Jor-**
13:11-12 **dan, and Lot journeyed east; and they separated**
themselves from each other. Abram dwelt in the
land of Canaan, and Lot dwelt in the cities of the
plain and moved his tent as far as Sodom.

[In Genesis 14], the fighting [among the kings] occurred mainly at Sodom…because one of God's people, Lot, was living there. Before the time of that fighting, Lot had separated himself from Abraham (13:11). Do you think that it was good for Lot to have separated himself from Abraham? No, it was not good. All of the young people today like to be separated from the older generation. In God's economy, however, it is not good for the young ones to be separated from the older generation. If you do this, you will miss the mark and the protection. At the time of Genesis 13, God's goal and eternal mark were with Abraham. If you had been there and had separated yourself from him, it would have been equal to separating yourself from God's mark. God's goal is with the called ones. If you separate yourself from the called ones, you separate yourself from God's goal. Lot should never have separated himself from Abraham, because God's goal was with Abraham. To leave Abraham was to leave God's mark. Moreover, to leave Abraham was to leave the protection. (*Life-study of Genesis*, p. 578)

Today's Reading

Lot was not firstly defeated by the four kings. That defeat was the issue of at least two foregoing defeats. Before Lot was captured by Chedorlaomer, he already had had two defeats. The first defeat occurred when Lot's herdsmen were striving against Abraham's herdsmen and Abraham offered Lot the choice of the land (Gen. 13:7-11). When Abraham offered the choice to Lot, Lot should have said, "Uncle, my choice is you. My choice is your choice. I don't like to make any choice of my own. If my herdsmen will not listen to me, I will fire them, but I will never go away from you. I have no choice but you and your choice." But, on the contrary, when Abraham gave him his choice, immediately, without much consideration, Lot made his choice and went his way. That was his first defeat.

After separating from Abraham, "Lot dwelt in the cities of the plain and moved his tent as far as Sodom" (13:12). Lot was going downhill. After taking the first step downward, it was easy for him to take the second and the third. The first step was leaving Abraham, who stood afar off from Sodom. Lot took the way that was toward Sodom. He walked in the direction of Sodom. In the eyes of God, Sodom was a wicked and sinful city (13:13). Lot, as one of the people of God, surely knew this. He should have stayed away from Sodom and not have walked towards it. Nevertheless, because the land around Sodom was rich, Lot journeyed toward Sodom. Eventually, he moved into the city, lived there, and settled there. That was his second defeat.

Do you think that God will allow His people to dwell in such a wicked city? Certainly not. Thus, under God's sovereignty, Chedorlaomer led the attack against Sodom. God allowed that war to take place. Four kings fought against five kings. Humanly speaking, the five kings should have been victorious since their number was greater. But the four kings defeated the five kings, and the city of Sodom was taken. The Bible stresses the taking of Sodom because Lot dwelt there. This fighting was not merely a matter of four kings against five kings; it was a fighting for one of God's people. Lot might have been peaceful as he dwelt in Sodom, but God was not peaceful. God would never allow Lot to stay there in peace. God might have said, "Lot, you may have peace within, but I will stir up some disturbance from without. I will send the four kings to defeat the five kings and capture your city. They will capture you, your family, and all that you have." This is in fact what happened to Lot. Lot suffered defeat after defeat. Eventually, as the last step of his defeat, he fell into the hands of the enemy. He was captured, and the king of Sodom could not help him. (*Life-study of Genesis,* pp. 578-579)

Further Reading: Life-study of Genesis, msg. 42

Enlightenment and inspiration: _____

_____

_____

_____

Morning Nourishment

**Gen. And when Abram heard that his brother had been
14:14-16 taken captive, he led out his trained men, born in
his house, three hundred eighteen *of them*, and
pursued as far as Dan. And he...struck them....
And he brought back all the possessions and also
brought back Lot his brother and his possessions
as well as the women and the people.**

In the matter of the capture of Lot, God was sovereign. Genesis 14:13 says, "And one who had escaped came and told Abram the Hebrew."...While so many others were captured, this one escaped. That person was preserved by God's sovereignty. As we shall see, it must have happened because of the intercession behind the scene.

Unlike us, Abraham did not count the weak point of his brother and did not take pleasure in Lot's suffering and calamity. Abraham did not say, "Lot should never have separated himself from me. I knew this was going to happen. He got what he deserved. I believe that God is sovereign and that Lot's suffering comes from God. Be at peace and go home. God will preserve Lot."...When he received this information, he made a strong decision to fight for Lot (14:14)....In verse 22 [Abraham] told the king of Sodom that before he went out to war he lifted up his hand to God. How could Abraham have prayed and made such a decision? It must have been due to the fact that someone behind the scene was interceding for him....As a result of this intercession, Abraham made a brief and bold decision. (*Life-study of Genesis,* pp. 579-580)

Today's Reading

Abraham decided to take his three hundred eighteen men and fight against the four kings and their armies....How could Abraham have fought against them with such a small number? Moreover, they were kings and generals who had fought many battles, and Abraham was a layman. How could he fight against those who were experts in war?...Nevertheless, Abraham was bold, having confidence in God.

Abraham's bold decision must have been due to the fact that behind the scene someone was interceding for him. Perhaps you are thinking that there is no record of this in the Bible. Neither is there a record of Melchizedek's parents or genealogy. But do you believe that he had no parents or genealogy? Certainly he did, yet the Bible does not mention them. Many things behind the scene in this chapter are not recorded....Someone concerned for God's interest on earth was interceding for Lot, Abraham, and Abraham's fighting.

Then the time came when Abraham could show the whole universe that he was on God's side. When Melchizedek appeared, two special titles of God are revealed: God the Most High and Possessor of heaven and earth (Gen. 14:19). Both Melchizedek and Abraham spoke of God in this way. Abraham said, "I have lifted up my hand to Jehovah, God the Most High, Possessor of heaven and earth" (14:22). Abraham could say, "By going down to Egypt I have learned the lesson that my God, the One who called me, is the Possessor of both heaven and earth. I don't need to have any choice. My choice is just He. I cannot bear seeing that my brother has been captured. This is a shame to me. I must take him back. I don't care for the number of soldiers and I don't care for the kings and armies....My burden is to get my brother back. If I don't do this, it is a shame to me."

It was not a small thing for him to risk his life in order to rescue his captured brother. But he did it. The fight went smoothly, and Abraham pursued the enemy from the south all the way to Dan in the north. His victory must have been the result of the intercession behind the scene.

Abraham gained the victory by trusting in God. He had confidence in God because he had learned to know Him. Likewise, we all must learn to know God. We must learn that, even today, the earth is God's. God is the landlord. He is not only the landlord but also the heavenlord. (*Life-study of Genesis,* pp. 580-582)

Further Reading: Truth Lessons—Level One, vol. 1, lsn. 8

Enlightenment and inspiration: _____

_____

_____

_____

Morning Nourishment

Gen.   And Melchizedek the king of Salem brought out
14:18-20 bread and wine. Now he was priest of God the Most
         High. And he blessed him and said, Blessed be
         Abram of God the Most High, Possessor of heaven
         and earth; and blessed be God the Most High, who
         has delivered your enemies into your hand...

Melchizedek is a type of Christ as the kingly High Priest (Heb. 7:1-3...). After Abraham gained the victory, Melchizedek appeared. Before his appearing, Melchizedek, a priest of God, must have been interceding for Abraham. It must have been through his intercession that Abraham was able to slaughter the four kings and gain the victory (cf. Exo. 17:8-13). Today Christ, our High Priest, is interceding for us in a hidden way (Rom. 8:34b; Heb. 7:25b) that we may be His overcomers to defeat God's enemies, so that through our victory Christ can be manifested openly in His second coming. (Gen. 14:18, footnote 1)

Today's Reading

[Melchizedek] is very much like Christ. When he came in, it signified that Christ came in. He was a type of Christ as God's High Priest. This is not revealed in Genesis 14, but it is found in Psalm 110. In Psalm 110 we are told that God's anointed One, the very Christ, is the Priest according to the order of Melchizedek, an order which is prior to that of Aaron. Before Aaron came into the priesthood, Melchizedek was God's Priest already.

The Aaronic priesthood dealt with sin, taking care of things on the negative side. The ministry of Melchizedek, on the contrary, is positive. Melchizedek did not come in to take away sin. He did not appear because Abraham had sinned but because Abraham had gained the victory. Melchizedek did not appear with an offering to take away sin but with bread and wine to nourish the victor....As such a High Priest, Christ does not take care of sin but ministers to us the processed God, signified by the bread and wine, as our nourishment.

While we walk on this earth, many things happen to us.

Apparently, these things just happen. Actually, behind the earthly scene, an intercession is going on. Our Melchizedek, our High Priest Christ, is still interceding for us in heaven (Heb. 7:25). His intercession overshadows us and cares for us.

We need to slaughter some kings daily. We need to slaughter the kings in our mind, emotion, and will. We need to slaughter the kings in our environment, families, and schools. After we have finished our slaughter of the kings, our Melchizedek will come to us, meet with us, and celebrate our victory. The Lord will not come back until we have slaughtered all the kings. Then He will return and drink the fruit of the vine with us, as indicated by His word in Matthew 26:29: "I shall by no means drink of this product of the vine from now on until that day when I drink it new with you in the kingdom of My Father."

To us, the overcomers, Christ's second appearing will not be a surprise, but to the worldly people it will be a great surprise. They may say, "Who is this one? What is his name and where does he come from?" We may answer, "His name is Christ, the real Melchizedek, and He comes from the heavens where He has been interceding for centuries."

We all need to echo the Lord's intercession. If we turn to our spirit and contact Him, there will always be some echoing. If we go according to that echoing, forgetting our environment, enemies, and even ourselves, we shall gain the victory and slaughter the kings. At the end of our slaughter of all the kings, our Melchizedek will appear to us. That will be the second coming of Christ. When Christ comes in, the whole earth will know the Most High God. Then all the earth will realize that God is the Possessor of heaven and earth. The earth is not possessed by any king, president, statesman, or politician; it is possessed by God the Most High, the Possessor of heaven and earth. How can this fact be declared to the earth? Only by our slaughter of the kings. (*Life-study of Genesis,* pp. 583-585)

Further Reading: Life-study of Genesis, msg. 43

Enlightenment and inspiration: _____

_____

_____

_____

Morning Nourishment

Heb. If indeed then perfection were through the Levit-
7:11 ical priesthood..., what need was there still that a
different Priest should arise according to the order
of Melchizedek and that He should not be said *to be*
according to the order of Aaron?
25 Hence also He is able to save to the uttermost those
who come forward to God through Him, since He
lives always to intercede for them.

The priesthood of Melchizedek is mentioned in the Scriptures before the priesthood of Aaron (Exo. 28:1). The priesthood according to the order of Melchizedek is higher than the Aaronic priesthood (Heb. 7). In His earthly ministry Christ was a High Priest according to the order of Aaron for the putting away of sin (Heb. 9:14, 26). Then, in His heavenly ministry Christ was designated a High Priest according to the order of Melchizedek (Heb. 5:6, 10), not to offer sacrifices for sin but to minister to us the very God who was processed through incarnation, human living, crucifixion, and resurrection, signified by the bread and the wine (Matt. 26:26-28), as our life supply that we may be saved to the uttermost (Heb. 7:25a). (Gen. 14:18, footnote 3)

Today's Reading

This High Priest is of another order, not of the order of Aaron but of the order of Melchizedek. Melchizedek was a king, and his name means the king of righteousness. In Isaiah 32:1 we see that the title, king of righteousness, also refers to the Lord Jesus. Christ is the King of righteousness, today's Melchizedek. As the King of righteousness, Christ has made all things right with God and with one another. He has reconciled man to God and has appeased God for man. Righteousness issues in peace (Isa. 32:17). By His righteousness Christ has brought forth the fruit of peace.

Melchizedek is also the king of Salem, which means the king of peace, signifying that Christ is also the King of peace (Isa. 9:6). As the King of peace through righteousness, Christ has brought in peace between God and us. In peace He fulfills the ministry of His priesthood, ministering God to us for our enjoyment.

Christ is the High Priest, but His status is that of a king. As He functions as a Priest, He is a King. He is the King to be the Priest; so His priesthood is kingly, royal (1 Pet. 2:9). He combines the kingship together with the priesthood (Zech. 6:13) for God's building and for His glory. Christ's kingship maintains a peaceful order through righteousness. This peaceful order is necessary for God's building. The building of God's house is in a situation of peace. Christ's priesthood ministers all the supply needed for the building of God. In this His glory is manifested.

As you are fighting during the day, slaughtering the negative things, Christ, the High Priest, is interceding for you. This is clearly mentioned in Hebrews 7:25. At the end of the day, when you have finished your fighting and He has finished His interceding, He comes to you with bread and wine to have a good time with you. This is our High Priest. While the victor was fighting, Melchizedek was watching and interceding. He saw Abraham's victory and knew when to come with the bread and wine....The ministering Melchizedek must also have been the interceding high priest. This is the kind of High Priest that we have today in Christ.

Before our Melchizedek ministers the processed God to us, He intercedes for us, praying that we may take up our sword and slaughter the enemies. We must slaughter the self, the natural mind, the wild emotion, the stubborn will, and other enemies.... After we have finished our slaughtering, He will change His interceding to the ministering of bread and wine. The proper Christian life is to slaughter the enemies during the day and to enjoy the ministry of our Melchizedek with the bread and wine in the evening. At the end of every day, when the slaughtering and interceding have been accomplished, He and we, we and He, may have a good time enjoying the bread and wine in righteousness and peace. (*Life-study of Hebrews,* pp. 361-364)

Further Reading: Life-study of Hebrews, msg. 32

Enlightenment and inspiration: _____

_____

_____

_____

Morning Nourishment

Psa. **Your people will offer themselves willingly in the**
110:3-4 **day of Your warfare, in the splendor of *their* conse-**
cration. Your young men will be to You like the dew
from the womb of the dawn. Jehovah has sworn,
and He will not change: You are a Priest forever
according to the order of Melchizedek.

[In Psalm 110:3a], literally, the Hebrew words translated "offer themselves willingly" mean "be freewill offerings." Instead of the word *warfare,* some translations render the Hebrew word as "army" or "war." These different renderings all indicate that some kind of fighting is raging on. Today is still a time of fighting because Christ still does not have a footstool. Hence, this ministry is engaged in a constant struggle. We stand against and annul every kind of improper ground concerning the church, whether Catholic or Protestant, and this causes opposition and fighting. (*Life-study of the Psalms,* pp. 433-434)

Today's Reading

Do you realize that in the eyes of the Lord our willing consecration, our offering ourselves to Him, is a kind of splendor? Although the church has become degraded, throughout the centuries there has been a line of those who have offered themselves willingly to the Lord in the splendor, the beauty, of their consecration. Giving up everything on earth, thousands have offered themselves freely to Christ, and with this offering there was the splendor of consecration. John Nelson Darby was such a person. Darby lived to be eighty-one years of age and, because of his love for Christ, he never married. One day, in his old age, he was staying alone in a hotel and he said, "Lord Jesus, I still love You." No doubt, Darby was a freewill offering to the Lord in the splendor of consecration.

Instead of the word *splendor* some versions use the word *adornment.* The splendor of consecration is an adornment. We need to be adorned by offering ourselves willingly to the Lord. If we do this, we will be beautified with a divine, heavenly splendor.

[Psalm 110:3b] indicates that, on the one hand, Christ likes to see the splendor of our consecration; on the other hand, He desires the dew that comes from the womb of the morning. Christ enjoys seeing the splendor of those who offer themselves to Him as freewill offerings, but, even more important, He still needs some dew to water Him. Even Christ needs the watering. He needs us to be the dew that waters Him.

According to the poetry here, this dew comes from "the womb of the dawn." We need to enter into this womb to be conceived as the dew with which to water Christ. I believe that this involves the morning watch. If we do not rise up early in the morning, we will miss the opportunity to enter into the womb of the morning to be made dew for Christ's watering. Instead of being watered, He will be dry and we also will be dry. I hope that we all, especially the young people, will see that here Christ likens Himself to a plant that needs the mild, soft, gentle dew. May we respond to Him by saying, "Lord Jesus, I want to be the dew conceived and produced by the womb of the morning for You to be watered."

The Hebrew word translated "change" [in verse 4] may also be rendered "repent." Christ is not only the King with power and authority, as indicated in verse 2; He is also the High Priest, as revealed [here]. Today we need Christ not only as our King but also as our Priest to pray for us and to take care of our case before God.

Christ's ministry is of two sections. The first section was His ministry on earth, and the second section is His ministry in the heavens. In His earthly ministry He did many things. Now, having completed the first section of His ministry, Christ in His ascension is carrying out the second, the heavenly, section of His ministry. This includes both His kingship and His priesthood. As the King He has the scepter signifying power and authority to rule over the earth and to manage our affairs, and as the High Priest He is praying for us and taking care of our case. (*Life-study of the Psalms,* pp. 434-435)

Further Reading: Life-study of the Psalms, msg. 38

Enlightenment and inspiration: _____

_____

_____

_____

Morning Nourishment

Gen. **But Abram said to the king of Sodom, I have lifted**
14:22-23 **up my hand to Jehovah, God the Most High, Pos-**
sessor of heaven and earth, that I will not take a
thread or a sandal thong or anything that is yours,
lest you say, I have made Abram rich.

After Abraham brought back all the goods, including his
nephew Lot and his goods and the women and the people, the
king of Sodom went out to meet him at the valley of Shaveh.
Melchizedek king of Salem also brought forth bread and wine
to meet him. "And the king of Sodom said to Abram, Give me
the people, and take the possessions for yourself" (Gen. 14:21).
Abraham had learned the lesson. He did not consider the goods
as trophies of his hard-fought battle and that he deserved
them. On the contrary, [as seen] in verses 22-23...he took a certain stand and showed others that, other than Jehovah, no one
could give him anything. (*CWWN*, vol. 35, pp. 42-43)

Today's Reading

Abraham called God the "Possessor of heaven and earth" [Gen.
14:22]!...This means that because of Abraham's stand for the
Lord, heaven became the Lord's, and the earth became the Lord's.
God was no longer the Lord of heaven only, but the Possessor of
heaven and earth! Abraham did not invent the title *Possessor of
heaven and earth;* he learned this from Melchizedek. After he
slaughtered Chedorlaomer and the other kings, he met Melchizedek at the valley of Shaveh, which was the king's dale. After
he won the victory, he did not meet others at the height of the city
wall, but at the bottom of a humble valley. Melchizedek came to
him with bread and wine and blessed him, saying, "Blessed be
Abram of God the Most High, / Possessor of heaven and earth; /
And blessed be God the Most High, / Who has delivered your enemies into your hand" (vv. 19-20). Because a man stood on earth for
God, Melchizedek was able to proclaim God as the Possessor of
heaven and earth. This is the first time in the Bible that God was
called the Possessor of heaven and earth.

Abraham had passed through all the tests. In the end he overcame! This was God's work on Abraham. Blessed be the most high God, the Possessor of heaven and earth! (*CWWN,* vol. 35, "The God of Abraham, Isaac, and Jacob," p. 43)

Abraham's victory regulated and restituted the whole situation and rearranged the entire environment. The four kings had defeated the five kings and had captured everything. The whole situation had been turned upside down. Abraham's victory changed this situation altogether, turning it right side up. He turned the unjust environment into a just one and made the whole situation peaceful. As a result, there was the king of righteousness and the king of peace. Abraham's victory stopped all the fighting and strife and brought in genuine peace.

The king of Sodom could humbly, honestly, and truthfully say to Abraham, "You have gained the victory. Everything that you brought back must be yours. You take it. All I want is my people." If you and I had been Abraham, we probably would have said, "That is right and fair. I rescued your people and recovered everything that you lost. It is good that you have the people and that everything else be mine." But the environment that was rearranged by Abraham's victory was not at all like this. It was pure. Abraham said to the king of Sodom, "I will not take a thread or a sandal thong or anything that is yours, lest you say, I have made Abram rich" (14:23). Abraham seemed to be saying, "If I take a thread from you, you will be able to say that you have made me rich. But I want to give a full testimony to the whole universe that my riches do not come from you. My riches come from the Possessor of heaven and earth, from my Most High God." How pure this was!...In that situation there was righteousness and peace....In a sense, it was like the millennial kingdom, full of righteousness and peace (Isa. 32:1, 16-18; Psa. 72:2-3, 7). (*Life-study of Genesis,* pp. 586-587)

Further Reading: CWWN, vol. 35, "The God of Abraham, Isaac, and Jacob," ch. 3

Enlightenment and inspiration: _____

_____

_____

_____

Hymns, #1111

1   Gathered at Thy table, Lord;
    Here the bread and wine are spread.
    Thou, our High Priest, present here;
    We, by Thee, are richly fed.
    Thou, Lord, our Melchisedec—
    We, the ones You come to feed;
    God to us to minister,
    Rich supply to us indeed.

2   From the slaughter of the kings
    Abram did return one night,
    O'er the foe victorious,
    With the spoils of the fight.
    On the way this One he met,
    Who for him did intercede;
    King of Righteousness and Peace
    Meeting Abram in his need.

3   We too, Lord, the kings have fought
    In the battle all day long;
    By Thine intercession, Lord,
    We are now victorious, strong.
    Round this table here we meet,
    We Thy church victorious,
    To enjoy the ministering
    Of the processed God to us.

4   We're not sinners, miserable;
    All our sins are history!
    Now to us, the fighters true,
    Is Thy priestly ministry.
    Gathered in thanksgiving, Lord,
    Now our hearts to Thee we raise;
    To our great Melchisedec,
    Render we our highest praise!

Composition for prophecy with main point and sub-points: _____

_____

_____

_____

_____

_____

_____

_____

_____

_____

_____

_____

_____

_____

_____

_____

_____

_____

_____

_____

_____

_____

_____

_____

_____

_____

_____

_____

_____

_____

_____

_____

The Allegory of the Two Women

Scripture Reading: Gen. 16:1—17:14; Gal. 4:21-31

Day 1 I. **Sarah and Hagar, the wife and the concubine of Abraham, are an allegory of two covenants— the covenant of promise and the covenant of law (Gen. 16:1-3; Gal. 4:24):**

   A. Sarah, the free woman, signifies the covenant of promise, which is related to the new testament, the covenant of grace (vv. 23-24; Gen. 12:7; 15:7-21):

      1. In that covenant God promised that He would give Abraham the seed, without having any intention that Abraham needed to do anything in order to have it; God would work something into him so that he might bring forth a seed to fulfill His purpose; this is grace (v. 4).

      2. Sarah, as the free woman, the proper wife of Abraham, is a symbol of this covenant of grace; she brought forth Isaac by God's grace.

      3. The produce of the promise of grace, which is Isaac, is the seed for the fulfillment of God's purpose (17:19; 21:12b).

Day 2 B. Hagar, the maidservant, signifies the covenant
&   of law (Gal. 4:24-25):
Day 3
      1. Hagar, Abraham's concubine, is a symbol of the law; by this we can see that the position of the law is the position of a concubine (Gen. 16:1-3).

      2. The covenant of law, symbolized by Hagar, brings God's chosen people into the slavery, the bondage, of the law, making them slaves under the law, separated from the grace of God (Gal. 4:25; 5:1, 4).

      3. Abraham's producing of Ishmael through Hagar symbolizes man's attempt to fulfill God's purpose by the effort of the flesh in

coordination with the law (Gen. 16:4, 15-16; Gal. 2:16; 4:23a).

  4. Abraham brought forth Ishmael through Hagar by his fleshly effort and not by God's grace; therefore, Ishmael, as the issue of man's fleshly effort according to the law, was rejected by God (Gen. 17:18-19; 21:10; Gal. 4:30).

C. The promise was given in Genesis 12:2, 7; 13:15-17; and 15:4-5, and the covenant was made in 15:7-21:

  1. According to God's intention, the covenant of promise came first, before the covenant of law; He had no intention of bringing in the law and of having man endeavor to keep it for the fulfillment of His purpose.

  2. What God originally intended to do was to work Himself into man to fulfill His purpose through man (v. 4).

Day 4

D. The covenant that God made with Abraham in Genesis 15:7-21 was confirmed in Genesis 17:1-14 with circumcision:

  1. In verse 1 God revealed Himself to Abraham as the All-sufficient God; as the all-sufficient Mighty One, He is the source of grace to supply His called ones with the riches of His divine being so that they may bring forth Christ as the seed for the fulfillment of His purpose.

  2. In Genesis 16 Abraham exercised his flesh to produce Ishmael; in Genesis 17 God charged Abraham to cut off his flesh, to terminate his natural strength, so that God could come in and bring forth Isaac by His grace.

  3. The spiritual meaning of circumcision is to put off the flesh, to put off the self and the old man, through the crucifixion of Christ (Col. 2:11, 13a; Phil. 3:3):

    a. Spiritual circumcision is the constant application of Christ's death to our flesh (Gal. 5:24; Rom. 8:13).

b. Circumcision deals with the flesh that tries to do God's will and to fulfill His promise by itself; the significance of circumcision is to cut off the confidence of the flesh (Phil. 3:3).

4. The confirmation of the covenant with circumcision concerns the seed and the land for the fulfillment of God's purpose (Gen. 17:2-8):

a. In order to fulfill God's eternal purpose that man express and represent Him, we need to have Christ as our seed and as our land, and for this we need to be circumcised and to live a crucified life (Gal. 5:24; 6:14).

b. When the flesh, the self, and the old man have been terminated, the door is open for God to come in and bring forth Isaac (Gen. 18:10, 14; 21:1-3).

Day 5 II. **We need to consider Galatians 4:21-31 in the light of Abraham's experience in Genesis:**

A. In Galatians 4:21-31 Paul tells us that Hagar signifies the law, symbolized by the earthly Jerusalem, and that Sarah signifies grace, symbolized by the heavenly Jerusalem (vv. 25-26).

B. Hagar and Sarah represent two covenants—the covenant of law and the covenant of grace; the law is a matter of man's labor with man's ability to produce something, whereas grace is God given to His chosen people to produce the many sons (3:26; 4:6).

C. The original covenant that God made with Abraham was the covenant of grace:

1. In this covenant there is not the need for man's ability or effort but the need for God's grace to produce the many sons (3:29).

2. This covenant equals the new testament; this means that the covenant that God made with Abraham was actually the new testament (v. 8; Heb. 8:7-8):

      a. The new testament is a continuation of the covenant that God made with Abraham (Gen. 15:7-21).

      b. The new testament is a full continuation of the covenant of grace that God made with Abraham to produce sons; the first of the sons produced by this covenant was Abraham himself (Gal. 3:26; 4:6; Heb. 2:10).

D. The two kinds of children brought forth by the two covenants are different in their natures (Gal. 4:24, 28-31):

  1. Those brought forth by the covenant of law are born according to the flesh, and those brought forth by the covenant of promise are born according to the Spirit (v. 29).

  2. The children born according to the flesh have no right to participate in God's promised blessing, but the children born according to the Spirit have the full right (vv. 30-31).

  3. Because we have grace, Christ, and the life-giving Spirit, we are children according to the Spirit (6:18; Col. 1:27; 1 Cor. 15:45b):

      a. This Spirit is now in our spirit and makes us children according to the Spirit; this is the marvelous revelation in Galatians 3 and 4.

      b. As those who are children according to the Spirit, we should remain in the fulfillment of God's desire, enjoying grace, Christ, and the all-inclusive Spirit as the blessing of the gospel (3:14).

Day 6   E. Galatians 4 reveals that the mother of the believers, who is the Jerusalem above, the New Jerusalem, is the new covenant of grace symbolized by Sarah (v. 26):

  1. The New Jerusalem, the heavenly Jerusalem, the Jerusalem above, is our mother, and this mother is the new covenant of grace (Heb. 8:7-13; 12:22-23):

    a. The new covenant is our mother because it brought us forth as children of freedom (Gal. 4:31).

    b. We have been born under the new covenant, and the Jerusalem above is our mother (v. 26).

    c. This woman is the new covenant and our mother, and our mother is the grace of God.

2. The Father is the Grace-giver; the grace is the covenant; the covenant is the city, the Jerusalem above, the New Jerusalem, who is our mother; the sons produced by the mother are the components of the mother; and the mother returns to the Father to be one with Him, having come out from the Father and then going back to the Father as the destination (1:3; 1 Cor. 8:6).

3. To receive the new covenant and to keep it is to come to the heavenly Jerusalem and to the church; the new covenant, the heavenly Jerusalem, and the church are one (Heb. 8:7-13; 12:22-23).

4. The mother of the believers is the city for which Abraham was waiting (11:10):

    a. This city is identified in 12:22, which tells us that we have come forward to the heavenly Jerusalem, the wife of Christ and the mother of the New Testament believers, composed of the sons of God, who have been born of her.

    b. In choosing Abraham, God's intention was to carry out His economy, which is to produce many sons, brought forth by grace, to constitute the New Jerusalem—His ultimate and eternal corporate expression (Rev. 21:1-2, 7).

Morning Nourishment

Gal. **For it is written that Abraham had two sons,**
4:22-24 **one of the maidservant and one of the free**
woman. However the one of the maidser-
vant was born according to the flesh, but
the one of the free woman *was born* **through**
promise. These things are spoken allegori-
cally, for these women are two covenants...

Sarah, the freewoman, signifies the covenant of promise (Gal. 4:23). God's covenant of promise with Abraham was a covenant of grace. In that covenant God promised that He would give Abraham the seed, without having any intention that Abraham needed to do anything in order to have it. God would work something into him that he might bring forth a seed to fulfill His purpose. It would be God's doing, not Abraham's. This is grace. Sarah, as the free woman, the proper wife of Abraham, was a symbol of this covenant of grace. She brought forth Isaac not by man's strength but by God's grace. (*Life-study of Genesis,* p. 620)

Today's Reading

The seed for the fulfillment of God's purpose is nothing less than Christ Himself wrought by God into, through, and out of us. What God has wrought into us brings in Christ as the seed (Gal. 3:16). This seed will eventually become our land....Within we have Christ as the seed by whom we live, and without we have Christ as the land in whom we live. This is the church life with Christ as our life. This is the only way for us to fulfill God's purpose. (*Life-study of Genesis,* p. 625)

God ordained that Abraham would beget a son through Sarah. Galatians 4:23 tells us that "the one of the free woman was born through promise." The free woman was Sarah. Hagar represents the law, while Sarah represents grace....Doing things by ourselves is law, while grace is God doing things for us. Simply put, grace is God doing everything for us. If we are doing it, it is not grace. Only when God is doing it for us is it grace. Grace, as defined in the Bible, is not forbearance or tolerance, nor is it doing anything by ourselves. It is something specific that God does in us. The specific work God wanted to do in Abraham was begetting Isaac through Sarah. Isaac was to be begotten of Abraham, but he was to be begotten through grace and through God's promise.

Since Abraham wanted a son, he should have realized that God is the Father and should have allowed Him to be the Father, laying himself aside. Abraham wanted Isaac, but he should not have tried to beget him by himself. In other words, if we want Christ to inherit the land and if we want to stand for God, we should not try to bring Him in by ourselves. We should not act or do anything by ourselves. We have to put ourselves aside. This is the greatest and hardest test. This is where God's servants most frequently fail. We must remember that God's work must not only be free from sin; it must be free from our own efforts as well. God is not only asking how well a work is done, but who is doing the work. Unfortunately, it is easy to exhort men to forsake sin, but it is not easy to exhort men to forsake self-effort. May God bring us to the point where we can say to the Lord, "I want to do Your will! You are within me and You must enable me to do Your will. I am not here to do Your will by myself! It must be You, not I!"

The only thing that will satisfy His heart is that which is done by Himself alone. Although He has lowered Himself and is willing to use us, we have to remember that we are merely servants whom He uses as vessels in His hand. We cannot replace Him in anything. We can only allow God to work through us; we cannot do anything by ourselves. Eventually, Isaac was born of Abraham, but Isaac was the son born according to God's promise. It was God who caused Isaac to be born. God begot this son through Abraham. The principle of promise is totally different from the principle of Ishmael. May the Lord be merciful to us and deliver us from the principle of Ishmael. (*CWWN,* vol. 35, pp. 57, 55-56)

Further Reading: Life-study of Genesis, msg. 46; *CWWN,* vol. 35, "The God of Abraham, Isaac, and Jacob," ch. 4; *Truth Lessons— Level Three,* vol. 1, lsn. 6

Enlightenment and inspiration: _____

_____

_____

Morning Nourishment

Gal. **Now this Hagar is Sinai the mountain in Arabia**
4:25 **and corresponds to the Jerusalem which now is,**
for she is in slavery with her children.

5:1 *It is* **for freedom** *that* **Christ has set us free; stand**
fast therefore, and do not be entangled with a yoke
of slavery again.

Hagar, the bondwoman, signifies the covenant of law (Gal.
4:25)....When man is ignorant of God's grace, he will always
endeavor to do something to please God, and this brings in the
law, of which Hagar, the bondwoman, the improper wife of
Abraham, was the symbol. Since she was the improper wife,
she should not have come in. What she brought forth could not
remain in God's economy. This signifies that the law should
not have come in and that the produce of the law has no position in fulfilling God's purpose. Hagar brought forth Ishmael,
who was rejected by God, by man's effort, not by God's grace.
The produce of man's effort through the law has no share in the
fulfillment of God's purpose. (*Life-study of Genesis*, p. 620)

Today's Reading

According to God's economy, a man should only have one
wife. Thus, Sarah's proposal that Abraham have a seed by
Hagar was absolutely against God's economy. Hagar was not a
proper wife but a concubine. Hagar, Abraham's concubine, was
a symbol of the law. By this we can see that the position of the
law is the position of the concubine. While grace is the proper
wife, the mother of the proper heirs (Gal. 4:26, 28, 31), the law is
the concubine, the mother of those who are rejected as heirs.
According to the ancient custom, men mainly took concubines
because their wives could not bear children. This is quite
meaningful. When grace has not yet worked and you are in a
hurry, you will join yourself to a concubine, to the law. Sarah
was a symbol of grace, of the covenant of promise, and Hagar was
a symbol of the law. Grace is the proper wife and the law is the
concubine.

Without exception, every Christian is like Abraham. After we were saved, we came to realize that God wants us to live a Christ-like life, a heavenly life, a victorious life, a life that constantly pleases God and glorifies Him. Yes, God does want us to live such a life, but He will work Christ into us to live for us a heavenly life to please Him and glorify Him. However, all of us focus on the intention and neglect the grace. The intention is that we live a heavenly life for the glory of God, and the grace is that God will work Christ into us for the fulfillment of His purpose. So firstly we rely upon our Lot, that which we brought with us from our natural background, trying to use him to fulfill God's purpose in living a heavenly life for the glory of God. When God does not allow us to rely upon Lot, then we turn to Eliezer, expecting that he will enable us to live a heavenly life for God's glory. Eventually God tells us, "I don't want that. I don't want anything objective but something subjective from within your own being." Once we realize that God wants this, then we begin to exercise our own energy, our natural strength, to fulfill God's purpose. We all have a Hagar, a maid who is always willing to cooperate with us. We may not have the law given by Moses, but we do have many self-made laws. We all are lawgivers and make laws for ourselves.

Whether we succeed or not in keeping our laws makes no difference in the eyes of God because in His eyes even our successes do not count. In the past years some sisters nearly succeeded in fulfilling their self-made laws. They had a strong character, a strong will, and a strong intention, and all day long they tried their best to control their temper and to be nice, sweet, and humble. Although such sisters might have been successful at this, what they produced was just an Ishmael. These sisters were happy with their Ishmael and, in a sense, they were proud of him. The principle is exactly the same with the brothers. (*Life-study of Genesis,* pp. 620-622)

Further Reading: Life-study of Genesis, msg. 46

Enlightenment and inspiration: _____

_____

_____

_____

Morning Nourishment

Gal. You have been brought to nought, *separated* from
5:4 Christ, you who are being justified by law; you
    have fallen from grace.
4:30 ..."Cast out the maidservant and her son, for the
    son of the maidservant shall by no means inherit
    with the son of the free woman."

The New Testament tells us that after we are saved we need
to preach the gospel and bear fruit. But how much natural
effort and strength are exercised in the matter of so-called soul
winning! Many kinds of Hagars, all of whom were acquired in
Egypt, are used to win souls. Every worldly means of soul-
winning is a Hagar. Yes, you may use Hagar to win souls, but
what kind of souls will you win? They will not be Isaac but
Ishmael. According to the New Testament, the proper fruit-
bearing and gospel preaching are by the overflow of the inner
life, by God working Christ into, through, and out of us. This
means that the proper gospel preaching is by Christ as grace to
us. (*Life-study of Genesis*, p. 623)

Today's Reading

As long as we still have the strength to produce an Ishmael,
God cannot do anything. After the producing of that Ishmael, He
will stay away for a period of time. When Abraham was ninety-
nine years of age, according to his figuration, he was a dead
person [cf. Rom. 4:19]....Romans 4 also indicates that Sarah was
out of function. Both Abraham and Sarah were fully convinced
that they were finished and could do nothing themselves. At
that point God came in.

All of the revival preachers stir up people, telling them to live
for Christ and to work for Him. But in our ministry we are
saying that you have to stop living a Christian life by yourselves
and doing a Christian work with worldly means. Do not be both-
ered at our saying this, for regardless how much we tell people to
stop, hardly anyone will stop....Although it is easy to be called
by God, it is most difficult to stop your natural zeal. If the Lord

would come in to stop you, you might say, "No, Lord. Look at today's situation. Hardly anyone works for You in what I am burdened to do. I'm nearly the only one. How could I stop my work for You?" But blessed is the one who will stop, for when you stop, God comes in. The end of humanity is the beginning of divinity. When our human life ends, the divine life begins.

When Abraham was eighty-six years of age, he still had too much of his own strength, causing God to wait for another thirteen years. Perhaps God, sitting in the heavens and looking at Abraham, said, "Abraham, you are now eighty-six, but I still have to wait for another thirteen years." While you are praying that God will do something, God is praying that you will stop. While you are saying, "O Lord, help me to do something," God is saying, "It would really be good for you to stop." While Abraham was so busy on earth, God might have looked at him and said, "Poor Abraham, you don't need to be that busy. Won't you stop and let Me come in? Please stop and let Me do it. Since you won't stop, I have to wait until you are ninety-nine years old." God waited until Abraham was a dying person out of function. Then He came in and could say, "Now is My start. Now is My time to begin something."

The produce of the effort of the flesh was Ishmael, but Ishmael was rejected by God (Gen. 17:18-19; 21:10-12a; Gal. 4:30). Not only was Ishmael rejected by God, but he also frustrated God's appearing. Our experience today tells us the same thing, for our Ishmael breaks our fellowship with God and keeps us from God's appearing....We must forget our doing and our working and take care of God's appearing. When God's appearing is with us, we are in the grace, in the covenant of grace. But most Christians today only care for their doing and work, not for God's appearing and presence....What we need is God's presence. What we need is not the outward fruit of our outward work but the inward appearing of our God. (*Life-study of Genesis*, pp. 623-625)

Further Reading: Life-study of Genesis, msg. 46; *Truth Lessons—Level Three*, vol. 1, lsn. 6

Enlightenment and inspiration: _____

_____

_____

_____

Morning Nourishment

Col.   In Him also you were circumcised with a circumci-
2:11 sion not made with hands, in the putting off of the
       body of the flesh, in the circumcision of Christ.
Phil. For we are the circumcision, the ones who serve by
3:3   the Spirit of God and boast in Christ Jesus and
       have no confidence in the flesh.

In order for us to have God added into us and to be broad-
ened we need to be circumcised. The covenant that God made
with Abraham in Genesis 15 was confirmed in Genesis 17 with
circumcision. There was no need for God to confirm it again, for
He had confirmed it once already, but it had to be confirmed
from Abraham's side. While God was faithful to His covenant,
Abraham was not because he had used his natural strength to
produce Ishmael. Since Abraham's use of his natural energy
with Hagar to produce Ishmael was the cause of the trouble,
God confirmed His covenant by having Abraham circumcised
(17:9-11, 13). (*Life-study of Genesis,* p. 636)

Today's Reading

In the New Testament we can find out the significance of circumcision....Circumcision is a matter of putting off the flesh,
the old man; it is not a matter of dealing with sin. In a strict
sense, circumcision has nothing to do with the dealing with sin;
it is a matter of being crucified and buried with Christ. Circumcision means to terminate your self, to terminate your flesh.
Abraham exercised his flesh in Genesis 16, but here, in Genesis 17, God wanted his flesh to be cut off. In Genesis 16 he had
energized his natural strength, but in Genesis 17 his strength
had to be terminated. This is circumcision.

The problem is the same today. As long as our natural
strength remains, it is difficult for God to come in to be our
everything for the fulfillment of His purpose. God wants to come
into us to be everything to us, but our flesh, our natural being
and strength, our old man and our old self, are a frustration to
God's being everything to us. This self, this old man, must be

terminated. It must be circumcised, that is, crucified. I want to tell you the good news that our old man has been crucified already (Rom. 6:6). With Abraham, it was to be crucified, but with us, it has been crucified already. We all must see this, reckon on it, and take it by faith. By faith we can declare that our flesh, our natural man with its strength, has been crucified. "I am crucified with Christ; and it is no longer I who live, but it is Christ who lives in me" (Gal. 2:20).We all need to live with the realization that the old man, the self, has been crucified. If we declare this and live according to it, then the God of resurrection immediately has the way to come into us and to be everything to us for the carrying out of His economy.

The confirmation of the covenant by circumcision concerned the seed and the land for the fulfillment of God's purpose (Gen. 17:2-8). In order to fulfill God's eternal purpose that man express and represent Him, we need to have Christ as our seed and as our land. In order to have Christ as the seed and the land for the fulfillment of God's purpose, we need to be circumcised and to live a crucified life. Circumcision is for the fulfillment of God's purpose. When the flesh, the self, and the old man have been terminated, the door is open for God to come in and bring forth Isaac.

All of the uncircumcised people were cut off from this covenant. In 17:14 God said to Abraham, "As for the uncircumcised male who is not circumcised in the flesh of his foreskin, that person shall be cut off from his people; he has broken My covenant." This is true today. If we do not live a crucified life, we are cut off from Christ, from the church life, and from the supply of the divine udder. Whenever we are unwilling to be circumcised, we are finished with the fulfilling of God's eternal purpose. Today our enjoying God, our living by Christ, and our practicing the church life all depend upon one thing—upon circumcision, upon living a crucified life. (*Life-study of Genesis,* pp. 636-638)

Further Reading: Life-study of Genesis, msg. 47; *CWWN,* vol. 35, "The God of Abraham, Isaac, and Jacob," ch. 5

Enlightenment and inspiration: _____

_____

_____

_____

Morning Nourishment

Gal. And the Scripture, foreseeing that God would jus-
3:8 tify the Gentiles out of faith, announced the gospel
beforehand to Abraham: "In you shall all the nations be blessed."
26 For you are all sons of God through faith in Christ
Jesus.

God's goal of bringing forth many sons is accomplished not by
man's work but by God's grace. What is God's grace? Contrary to
the concept of many, God's grace is not merely unmerited favor.
According to the divine revelation in the New Testament, grace
is actually God Himself given to His chosen people for their enjoyment, and this enjoyment will make them God's sons.

This understanding of the grace of God is found in the Gospel
of John. In John 1 we see that the Word, who is the very God, became flesh (vv. 1, 14) and that grace came with Him (v. 17). This
means that He came as grace. According to John 1, God came as
grace to be received by His chosen ones. Verses 12 and 13 say, "As
many as received Him, to them He gave the authority to become
children of God, to those who believe into His name, who were
begotten not of blood, nor of the will of the flesh, nor of the will of
man, but of God." Whoever believes in Him and receives Him
will be born of Him to become one of His children. Therefore, by
giving Himself to His chosen people as grace, God brings forth
many sons. (*The Conclusion of the New Testament*, p. 2668)

Today's Reading

God told Abraham to send Ishmael away, saying, "In Isaac
shall your seed be called" (Gen. 21:12). God never recognized
Ishmael as Abraham's heir, for He regarded Isaac as the unique
son. Isaac as the unique son of Abraham was brought forth
through God's grace, not through the natural ability of either
Abraham or Sarah. The producing of Isaac was altogether a
matter of God's grace, that is, of God Himself given to His chosen
people to produce His many sons. Ishmael, on the contrary, was
produced by Abraham's natural ability and strength.

Let us now consider Galatians 4 in the light of Abraham's experience in Genesis. In this chapter Paul tells us that Hagar signifies the law symbolized by the earthly Jerusalem and that Sarah signifies grace symbolized by the heavenly Jerusalem. Hence, Hagar and Sarah represent two covenants—the covenant of law and the covenant of grace. The law is a matter of man's labor with man's ability to produce something, whereas grace is God given to His chosen people to produce the many sons.

It was not God's intention to make a covenant of law with Abraham. The covenant of law was something additional; it was not the original covenant. The original covenant God made with Abraham was the covenant of grace. In this covenant there is not the need for man's ability or effort but the need for God's grace to produce the many sons. This covenant equals the new testament. This means that the covenant God made with Abraham was actually the new testament. The new testament is, therefore, a continuation of the covenant God made with Abraham. All of Abraham's genuine descendants, such as Isaac, Jacob, Moses, and David, were under this covenant, which is the covenant we are under today. They were not under the covenant of law. Although the covenant of law was given through Moses, he himself was not under that covenant. Rather, in the sight of God, Moses was under the covenant of grace. The covenant of law cannot produce anything for God; this covenant can only bring forth "Ishmaels."

The new testament is a full continuation of the covenant of grace God made with Abraham to produce sons. The first of the sons produced by this covenant was Abraham himself. Abraham is the father of all those who believe (Rom. 4:11). But this father was the first son produced by the covenant of grace. Other sons in the Old Testament include Jacob, David, and Jeremiah but not Esau. (*The Conclusion of the New Testament*, pp. 2670-2671)

Further Reading: The Conclusion of the New Testament, msg. 254; *Life-study of Galatians*, msgs. 25-26

Enlightenment and inspiration: _____

_____

_____

_____

Morning Nourishment

Gal. But the Jerusalem above is free, which is our
4:26 mother.
Heb. But you have come forward to Mount Zion and
12:22-23 to the city of the living God, the heavenly Jerusalem...and to the church of the firstborn...

Galatians 4:26-28 and 31 reveal that the New Jerusalem is
the mother of the believers. This mother is the Jerusalem above,
the heavenly Jerusalem. In Galatians 4 Hagar symbolizes the
old covenant of the law that condemns and brings in death, producing children unto slavery (vv. 24-25), whereas Sarah symbolizes the new covenant of grace that justifies and brings in life,
producing children unto freedom (vv. 26-28, 31). The New Jerusalem, the heavenly Jerusalem, the Jerusalem above, is our
mother, and this mother is the new covenant of grace. The new
covenant is our mother because it brought us forth as children of
freedom. (*The Conclusion of the New Testament,* p. 2673)

Today's Reading

The center of the New Jerusalem, which is the mother of the
believers, is God and the Lamb on the throne (Rev. 22:1). This is
the Triune God as the center and element of the mother of the
believers. The Triune God is also the element of the new covenant of grace. Grace is the processed Triune God for our enjoyment. Because the new covenant brings us God Himself for our
enjoyment, it is called the new covenant of grace. Furthermore,
the Triune God is the element, essence, and nature of the children of freedom. The Triune God is thus the element and substance of the components of the mother. Finally, the Triune God
is the center, substance, element, and essence of the ultimate
consummation of the Scriptures—the New Jerusalem.

To receive the new covenant and to keep it is to come to the
heavenly Jerusalem and to the church (Heb. 8:7-13; 12:22-23).
The new covenant, the heavenly Jerusalem, and the church are
one. In order to understand this we need to see the link between
Galatians and Hebrews. Galatians deals with Judaism, warning

the believers not to backslide into Judaism but to stay in grace. Hebrews charges us not to drift into the old covenant but to remain in the new covenant. Chapters seven through ten of Hebrews are on the better covenant, the new covenant. Hebrews 8 indicates that the old covenant is over and that the new covenant has come in to replace it. Then in Hebrews 12 Paul tells us that we have come to Mount Zion, to the city of the living God, and to the church (vv. 22-23).

To come to the new covenant is to come to the New Jerusalem. Without Galatians 4 as a background, it would be very difficult to understand this. Galatians 4 reveals that the mother of the believers, who is the Jerusalem above, the New Jerusalem, is the new covenant of grace symbolized by Sarah. To come to the new covenant is to come not only to the New Jerusalem but also to the church (Heb. 12:23). To keep the new covenant is to remain in the New Jerusalem. This indicates that we are not going to the New Jerusalem but that we are in the New Jerusalem already. The tense of the verb in Hebrews 12:22 is the perfect tense, "have come," not the future tense. We know that we have come to the New Jerusalem because the New Jerusalem is the new covenant. Because we have received the new covenant, we have entered into the New Jerusalem. The receiving of the new covenant is the entering into the New Jerusalem.

The New Jerusalem is the ultimate consummation of the Triune God passing through the long process of His new covenant. Without the Triune God, the new covenant would be an empty shell. The Triune God in His new covenant is dispensing Himself into us, making us the components of His ultimate consummation. Hence, the ultimate consummation will not be the Triune God alone; it will be the mingling of the processed Triune God with His redeemed, regenerated, and transformed tripartite people. This will be the New Jerusalem in the new heaven and new earth. (*The Conclusion of the New Testament,* pp. 2673-2675)

Further Reading: The Conclusion of the New Testament, msg. 255

Enlightenment and inspiration: _____

_____

_____

_____

Hymns, #497

1   Grace in its highest definition is
     God in the Son to be enjoyed by us;
     It is not only something done or giv'n,
     But God Himself, our portion glorious.

2   God is incarnate in the flesh that we
     Him may receive, experience ourself;
     This is the grace which we receive of God,
     Which comes thru Christ and which is Christ Himself.

3   Paul the Apostle counted all as dung,
     'Twas only God in Christ he counted grace;
     'Tis by this grace—the Lord experienced—
     That he surpassed the others in the race.

4   It is this grace—Christ as our inward strength—
     Which with His all-sufficiency doth fill;
     It is this grace which in our spirit is,
     There energizing, working out God's will.

5   This grace, which is the living Christ Himself,
     Is what we need and must experience;
     Lord, may we know this grace and by it live,
     Thyself increasingly as grace to sense.

Composition for prophecy with main point and sub-points: _____

_____

_____
_____
_____
_____
_____
_____
_____
_____
_____
_____
_____
_____
_____
_____
_____
_____
_____
_____
_____
_____
_____
_____
_____
_____
_____
_____
_____
_____
_____
_____
_____
_____
_____

Reading Schedule for the Recovery Version of the Old Testament with Footnotes

Wk.	Lord's Day	Monday	Tuesday	Wednesday	Thursday	Friday	Saturday
1	☐ Gen. 1:1-5	☐ 1:6-23	☐ 1:24-31	☐ 2:1-9	☐ 2:10-25	☐ 3:1-13	☐ 3:14-24
2	☐ 4:1-26	☐ 5:1-32	☐ 6:1-22	☐ 7:1—8:3	☐ 8:4-22	☐ 9:1-29	☐ 10:1-32
3	☐ 11:1-32	☐ 12:1-20	☐ 13:1-18	☐ 14:1-24	☐ 15:1-21	☐ 16:1-16	☐ 17:1-27
4	☐ 18:1-33	☐ 19:1-38	☐ 20:1-18	☐ 21:1-34	☐ 22:1-24	☐ 23:1—24:27	☐ 24:28-67
5	☐ 25:1-34	☐ 26:1-35	☐ 27:1-46	☐ 28:1-22	☐ 29:1-35	☐ 30:1-43	☐ 31:1-55
6	☐ 32:1-32	☐ 33:1—34:31	☐ 35:1-29	☐ 36:1-43	☐ 37:1-36	☐ 38:1—39:23	☐ 40:1—41:13
7	☐ 41:14-57	☐ 42:1-38	☐ 43:1-34	☐ 44:1-34	☐ 45:1-28	☐ 46:1-34	☐ 47:1-31
8	☐ 48:1-22	☐ 49:1-15	☐ 49:16-33	☐ 50:1-26	☐ Exo. 1:1-22	☐ 2:1-25	☐ 3:1-22
9	☐ 4:1-31	☐ 5:1-23	☐ 6:1-30	☐ 7:1-25	☐ 8:1-32	☐ 9:1-35	☐ 10:1-29
10	☐ 11:1-10	☐ 12:1-14	☐ 12:15-36	☐ 12:37-51	☐ 13:1-22	☐ 14:1-31	☐ 15:1-27
11	☐ 16:1-36	☐ 17:1-16	☐ 18:1-27	☐ 19:1-25	☐ 20:1-26	☐ 21:1-36	☐ 22:1-31
12	☐ 23:1-33	☐ 24:1-18	☐ 25:1-22	☐ 25:23-40	☐ 26:1-14	☐ 26:15-37	☐ 27:1-21
13	☐ 28:1-21	☐ 28:22-43	☐ 29:1-21	☐ 29:22-46	☐ 30:1-10	☐ 30:11-38	☐ 31:1-17
14	☐ 31:18—32:35	☐ 33:1-23	☐ 34:1-35	☐ 35:1-35	☐ 36:1-38	☐ 37:1-29	☐ 38:1-31
15	☐ 39:1-43	☐ 40:1-38	☐ Lev. 1:1-17	☐ 2:1-16	☐ 3:1-17	☐ 4:1-35	☐ 5:1-19
16	☐ 6:1-30	☐ 7:1-38	☐ 8:1-36	☐ 9:1-24	☐ 10:1-20	☐ 11:1-47	☐ 12:1-8
17	☐ 13:1-28	☐ 13:29-59	☐ 14:1-18	☐ 14:19-32	☐ 14:33-57	☐ 15:1-33	☐ 16:1-17
18	☐ 16:18-34	☐ 17:1-16	☐ 18:1-30	☐ 19:1-37	☐ 20:1-27	☐ 21:1-24	☐ 22:1-33
19	☐ 23:1-22	☐ 23:23-44	☐ 24:1-23	☐ 25:1-23	☐ 25:24-55	☐ 26:1-24	☐ 26:25-46
20	☐ 27:1-34	☐ Num. 1:1-54	☐ 2:1-34	☐ 3:1-51	☐ 4:1-49	☐ 5:1-31	☐ 6:1-27
21	☐ 7:1-41	☐ 7:42-88	☐ 7:89—8:26	☐ 9:1-23	☐ 10:1-36	☐ 11:1-35	☐ 12:1—13:33
22	☐ 14:1-45	☐ 15:1-41	☐ 16:1-50	☐ 17:1—18:7	☐ 18:8-32	☐ 19:1-22	☐ 20:1-29
23	☐ 21:1-35	☐ 22:1-41	☐ 23:1-30	☐ 24:1-25	☐ 25:1-18	☐ 26:1-65	☐ 27:1-23
24	☐ 28:1-31	☐ 29:1-40	☐ 30:1—31:24	☐ 31:25-54	☐ 32:1-42	☐ 33:1-56	☐ 34:1-29
25	☐ 35:1-34	☐ 36:1-13	☐ Deut. 1:1-46	☐ 2:1-37	☐ 3:1-29	☐ 4:1-49	☐ 5:1-33
26	☐ 6:1—7:26	☐ 8:1-20	☐ 9:1-29	☐ 10:1-22	☐ 11:1-32	☐ 12:1-32	☐ 13:1—14:21

Reading Schedule for the Recovery Version of the Old Testament with Footnotes

Wk.	Lord's Day	Monday	Tuesday	Wednesday	Thursday	Friday	Saturday
27	14:22—15:23 ☐	16:1-22 ☐	17:1—18:8 ☐	18:9—19:21 ☐	20:1—21:17 ☐	21:18—22:30 ☐	23:1-25 ☐
28	24:1-22 ☐	25:1-19 ☐	26:1-19 ☐	27:1-26 ☐	28:1-68 ☐	29:1-29 ☐	30:1—31:29 ☐
29	31:30—32:52 ☐	33:1-29 ☐	34:1-12 ☐	Josh. 1:1-18 ☐	2:1-24 ☐	3:1-17 ☐	4:1-24 ☐
30	5:1-15 ☐	6:1-27 ☐	7:1-26 ☐	8:1-35 ☐	9:1-27 ☐	10:1-43 ☐	11:1—12:24 ☐
31	13:1-33 ☐	14:1—15:63 ☐	16:1—18:28 ☐	19:1-51 ☐	20:1—21:45 ☐	22:1-34 ☐	23:1—24:33 ☐
32	Judg. 1:1-36 ☐	2:1-23 ☐	3:1-31 ☐	4:1-24 ☐	5:1-31 ☐	6:1-40 ☐	7:1-25 ☐
33	8:1-35 ☐	9:1-57 ☐	10:1—11:40 ☐	12:1—13:25 ☐	14:1—15:20 ☐	16:1-31 ☐	17:1—18:31 ☐
34	19:1-30 ☐	20:1-48 ☐	21:1-25 ☐	Ruth 1:1-22 ☐	2:1-23 ☐	3:1-18 ☐	4:1-22 ☐
35	1 Sam. 1:1-28 ☐	2:1-36 ☐	3:1—4:22 ☐	5:1—6:21 ☐	7:1—8:22 ☐	9:1-27 ☐	10:1—11:15 ☐
36	12:1—13:23 ☐	14:1-52 ☐	15:1-35 ☐	16:1-23 ☐	17:1-58 ☐	18:1-30 ☐	19:1-24 ☐
37	20:1-42 ☐	21:1—22:23 ☐	23:1—24:22 ☐	25:1-44 ☐	26:1-25 ☐	27:1—28:25 ☐	29:1—30:31 ☐
38	31:1-13 ☐	2 Sam. 1:1-27 ☐	2:1-32 ☐	3:1-39 ☐	4:1—5:25 ☐	6:1-23 ☐	7:1-29 ☐
39	8:1—9:13 ☐	10:1—11:27 ☐	12:1-31 ☐	13:1-39 ☐	14:1-33 ☐	15:1—16:23 ☐	17:1—18:33 ☐
40	19:1-43 ☐	20:1—21:22 ☐	22:1-51 ☐	23:1-39 ☐	24:1-25 ☐	1 Kings 1:1-19 ☐	1:20-53 ☐
41	2:1-46 ☐	3:1-28 ☐	4:1-34 ☐	5:1—6:38 ☐	7:1-22 ☐	7:23-51 ☐	8:1-36 ☐
42	8:37-66 ☐	9:1-28 ☐	10:1-29 ☐	11:1-43 ☐	12:1-33 ☐	13:1-34 ☐	14:1-31 ☐
43	15:1-34 ☐	16:1—17:24 ☐	18:1-46 ☐	19:1-21 ☐	20:1-43 ☐	21:1—22:53 ☐	2 Kings 1:1-18 ☐
44	2:1—3:27 ☐	4:1-44 ☐	5:1—6:33 ☐	7:1-20 ☐	8:1-29 ☐	9:1-37 ☐	10:1-36 ☐
45	11:1—12:21 ☐	13:1—14:29 ☐	15:1-38 ☐	16:1-20 ☐	17:1-41 ☐	18:1-37 ☐	19:1-37 ☐
46	20:1—21:26 ☐	22:1-20 ☐	23:1-37 ☐	24:1—25:30 ☐	1 Chron. 1:1-54 ☐	2:1—3:24 ☐	4:1—5:26 ☐
47	6:1-81 ☐	7:1-40 ☐	8:1-40 ☐	9:1-44 ☐	10:1—11:47 ☐	12:1-40 ☐	13:1—14:17 ☐
48	15:1—16:43 ☐	17:1-27 ☐	18:1—19:19 ☐	20:1—21:30 ☐	22:1—23:32 ☐	24:1—25:31 ☐	26:1-32 ☐
49	27:1-34 ☐	28:1—29:30 ☐	2 Chron. 1:1-17 ☐	2:1—3:17 ☐	4:1—5:14 ☐	6:1-42 ☐	7:1—8:18 ☐
50	9:1—10:19 ☐	11:1—12:16 ☐	13:1—15:19 ☐	16:1—17:19 ☐	18:1—19:11 ☐	20:1-37 ☐	21:1—22:12 ☐
51	23:1—24:27 ☐	25:1—26:23 ☐	27:1—28:27 ☐	29:1-36 ☐	30:1—31:21 ☐	32:1-33 ☐	33:1—34:33 ☐
52	35:1—36:23 ☐	Ezra 1:1-11 ☐	2:1-70 ☐	3:1—4:24 ☐	5:1—6:22 ☐	7:1-28 ☐	8:1-36 ☐

Reading Schedule for the Recovery Version of the Old Testament with Footnotes

Wk.	Lord's Day	Monday	Tuesday	Wednesday	Thursday	Friday	Saturday
53	☐ 9:1—10:44	☐ Neh. 1:1-11	☐ 2:1—3:32	☐ 4:1—5:19	☐ 6:1-19	☐ 7:1-73	☐ 8:1-18
54	☐ 9:1-20	☐ 9:21-38	☐ 10:1—11:36	☐ 12:1-47	☐ 13:1-31	☐ Esth. 1:1-22	☐ 2:1—3:15
55	☐ 4:1—5:14	☐ 6:1—7:10	☐ 8:1-17	☐ 9:1—10:3	☐ Job 1:1-22	☐ 2:1—3:26	☐ 4:1—5:27
56	☐ 6:1—7:21	☐ 8:1—9:35	☐ 10:1—11:20	☐ 12:1—13:28	☐ 14:1—15:35	☐ 16:1—17:16	☐ 18:1—19:29
57	☐ 20:1—21:34	☐ 22:1—23:17	☐ 24:1—25:6	☐ 26:1—27:23	☐ 28:1—29:25	☐ 30:1—31:40	☐ 32:1—33:33
58	☐ 34:1—35:16	☐ 36:1-33	☐ 37:1-24	☐ 38:1-41	☐ 39:1-30	☐ 40:1-24	☐ 41:1-34
59	☐ 42:1-17	☐ Psa. 1:1-6	☐ 2:1—3:8	☐ 4:1—6:10	☐ 7:1—8:9	☐ 9:1—10:18	☐ 11:1—15:5
60	☐ 16:1—17:15	☐ 18:1-50	☐ 19:1—21:13	☐ 22:1-31	☐ 23:1—24:10	☐ 25:1—27:14	☐ 28:1—30:12
61	☐ 31:1—32:11	☐ 33:1—34:22	☐ 35:1—36:12	☐ 37:1-40	☐ 38:1—39:13	☐ 40:1—41:13	☐ 42:1—43:5
62	☐ 44:1-26	☐ 45:1-17	☐ 46:1—48:14	☐ 49:1—50:23	☐ 51:1—52:9	☐ 53:1—55:23	☐ 56:1—58:11
63	☐ 59:1—61:8	☐ 62:1—64:10	☐ 65:1—67:7	☐ 68:1-35	☐ 69:1—70:5	☐ 71:1—72:20	☐ 73:1—74:23
64	☐ 75:1—77:20	☐ 78:1-72	☐ 79:1—81:16	☐ 82:1—84:12	☐ 85:1—87:7	☐ 88:1—89:52	☐ 90:1—91:16
65	☐ 92:1—94:23	☐ 95:1—97:12	☐ 98:1—101:8	☐ 102:1—103:22	☐ 104:1—105:45	☐ 106:1-48	☐ 107:1-43
66	☐ 108:1—109:31	☐ 110:1—112:10	☐ 113:1—115:18	☐ 116:1—118:29	☐ 119:1-32	☐ 119:33-72	☐ 119:73-120
67	☐ 119:121-176	☐ 120:1—124:8	☐ 125:1—128:6	☐ 129:1—132:18	☐ 133:1—135:21	☐ 136:1—138:8	☐ 139:1—140:13
68	☐ 141:1—144:15	☐ 145:1—147:20	☐ 148:1—150:6	☐ Prov. 1:1-33	☐ 2:1—3:35	☐ 4:1—5:23	☐ 6:1-35
69	☐ 7:1—8:36	☐ 9:1—10:32	☐ 11:1—12:28	☐ 13:1—14:35	☐ 15:1-33	☐ 16:1-33	☐ 17:1-28
70	☐ 18:1-24	☐ 19:1—20:30	☐ 21:1—22:29	☐ 23:1-35	☐ 24:1—25:28	☐ 26:1—27:27	☐ 28:1—29:27
71	☐ 30:1-33	☐ 31:1-31	☐ Eccl. 1:1-18	☐ 2:1—3:22	☐ 4:1—5:20	☐ 6:1—7:29	☐ 8:1—9:18
72	☐ 10:1—11:10	☐ 12:1-14	☐ S.S. 1:1-8	☐ 1:9-17	☐ 2:1-17	☐ 3:1-11	☐ 4:1-8
73	☐ 4:9-16	☐ 5:1-16	☐ 6:1-13	☐ 7:1-13	☐ 8:1-14	☐ Isa. 1:1-11	☐ 1:12-31
74	☐ 2:1-22	☐ 3:1-26	☐ 4:1-6	☐ 5:1-30	☐ 6:1-13	☐ 7:1-25	☐ 8:1-22
75	☐ 9:1-21	☐ 10:1-34	☐ 11:1—12:6	☐ 13:1-22	☐ 14:1-14	☐ 14:15-32	☐ 15:1—16:14
76	☐ 17:1—18:7	☐ 19:1-25	☐ 20:1—21:17	☐ 22:1-25	☐ 23:1-18	☐ 24:1-23	☐ 25:1-12
77	☐ 26:1-21	☐ 27:1-13	☐ 28:1-29	☐ 29:1-24	☐ 30:1-33	☐ 31:1—32:20	☐ 33:1-24
78	☐ 34:1-17	☐ 35:1-10	☐ 36:1-22	☐ 37:1-38	☐ 38:1—39:8	☐ 40:1-31	☐ 41:1-29

Reading Schedule for the Recovery Version of the Old Testament with Footnotes

Wk.	Lord's Day	Monday	Tuesday	Wednesday	Thursday	Friday	Saturday
79	42:1-25 ☐	43:1-28 ☐	44:1-28 ☐	45:1-25 ☐	46:1-13 ☐	47:1-15 ☐	48:1-22 ☐
80	49:1-13 ☐	49:14-26 ☐	50:1—51:23 ☐	52:1-15 ☐	53:1-12 ☐	54:1-17 ☐	55:1-13 ☐
81	56:1-12 ☐	57:1-21 ☐	58:1-14 ☐	59:1-21 ☐	60:1-22 ☐	61:1-11 ☐	62:1-12 ☐
82	63:1-19 ☐	64:1-12 ☐	65:1-25 ☐	66:1-24 ☐	Jer. 1:1-19 ☐	2:1-19 ☐	2:20-37 ☐
83	3:1-25 ☐	4:1-31 ☐	5:1-31 ☐	6:1-30 ☐	7:1-34 ☐	8:1-22 ☐	9:1-26 ☐
84	10:1-25 ☐	11:1—12:17 ☐	13:1-27 ☐	14:1-22 ☐	15:1-21 ☐	16:1—17:27 ☐	18:1-23 ☐
85	19:1—20:18 ☐	21:1—22:30 ☐	23:1-40 ☐	24:1—25:38 ☐	26:1—27:22 ☐	28:1—29:32 ☐	30:1-24 ☐
86	31:1-23 ☐	31:24-40 ☐	32:1-44 ☐	33:1-26 ☐	34:1-22 ☐	35:1-19 ☐	36:1-32 ☐
87	37:1-21 ☐	38:1-28 ☐	39:1—40:16 ☐	41:1—42:22 ☐	43:1—44:30 ☐	45:1—46:28 ☐	47:1—48:16 ☐
88	48:17-47 ☐	49:1-22 ☐	49:23-39 ☐	50:1-27 ☐	50:28-46 ☐	51:1-27 ☐	51:28-64 ☐
89	52:1-34 ☐	Lam. 1:1-22 ☐	2:1-22 ☐	3:1-39 ☐	3:40-66 ☐	4:1-22 ☐	5:1-22 ☐
90	Ezek. 1:1-14 ☐	1:15-28 ☐	2:1—3:27 ☐	4:1—5:17 ☐	6:1—7:27 ☐	8:1—9:11 ☐	10:1—11:25 ☐
91	12:1—13:23 ☐	14:1—15:8 ☐	16:1-63 ☐	17:1—18:32 ☐	19:1-14 ☐	20:1-49 ☐	21:1-32 ☐
92	22:1-31 ☐	23:1-49 ☐	24:1-27 ☐	25:1—26:21 ☐	27:1-36 ☐	28:1-26 ☐	29:1—30:26 ☐
93	31:1—32:32 ☐	33:1-33 ☐	34:1-31 ☐	35:1—36:21 ☐	36:22-38 ☐	37:1-28 ☐	38:1—39:29 ☐
94	40:1-27 ☐	40:28-49 ☐	41:1-26 ☐	42:1—43:27 ☐	44:1-31 ☐	45:1-25 ☐	46:1-24 ☐
95	47:1-23 ☐	48:1-35 ☐	Dan. 1:1-21 ☐	2:1-30 ☐	2:31-49 ☐	3:1-30 ☐	4:1-37 ☐
96	5:1-31 ☐	6:1-28 ☐	7:1-12 ☐	7:13-28 ☐	8:1-27 ☐	9:1-27 ☐	10:1-21 ☐
97	11:1-22 ☐	11:23-45 ☐	12:1-13 ☐	Hosea 1:1-11 ☐	2:1-23 ☐	3:1—4:19 ☐	5:1-15 ☐
98	6:1-11 ☐	7:1-16 ☐	8:1-14 ☐	9:1-17 ☐	10:1-15 ☐	11:1-12 ☐	12:1-14 ☐
99	13:1—14:9 ☐	Joel 1:1-20 ☐	2:1-16 ☐	2:17-32 ☐	3:1-21 ☐	Amos 1:1-15 ☐	2:1-16 ☐
100	3:1-15 ☐	4:1—5:27 ☐	6:1—7:17 ☐	8:1—9:15 ☐	Obad. 1-21 ☐	Jonah 1:1-17 ☐	2:1—4:11 ☐
101	Micah 1:1-16 ☐	2:1—3:12 ☐	4:1—5:15 ☐	6:1—7:20 ☐	Nahum 1:1-15 ☐	2:1—3:19 ☐	Hab. 1:1-17 ☐
102	2:1-20 ☐	3:1-19 ☐	Zeph. 1:1-18 ☐	2:1-15 ☐	3:1-20 ☐	Hag. 1:1-15 ☐	2:1-23 ☐
103	Zech. 1:1-21 ☐	2:1-13 ☐	3:1-10 ☐	4:1-14 ☐	5:1—6:15 ☐	7:1—8:23 ☐	9:1-17 ☐
104	10:1—11:17 ☐	12:1—13:9 ☐	14:1-21 ☐	Mal. 1:1-14 ☐	2:1-17 ☐	3:1-18 ☐	4:1-6 ☐

Reading Schedule for the Recovery Version of the New Testament with Footnotes

Wk.	Lord's Day	Monday	Tuesday	Wednesday	Thursday	Friday	Saturday
1	Matt. 1:1-2 ☐	1:3-7 ☐	1:8-17 ☐	1:18-25 ☐	2:1-23 ☐	3:1-6 ☐	3:7-17 ☐
2	4:1-11 ☐	4:12-25 ☐	5:1-4 ☐	5:5-12 ☐	5:13-20 ☐	5:21-26 ☐	5:27-48 ☐
3	6:1-8 ☐	6:9-18 ☐	6:19-34 ☐	7:1-12 ☐	7:13-29 ☐	8:1-13 ☐	8:14-22 ☐
4	8:23-34 ☐	9:1-13 ☐	9:14-17 ☐	9:18-34 ☐	9:35—10:5 ☐	10:6-25 ☐	10:26-42 ☐
5	11:1-15 ☐	11:16-30 ☐	12:1-14 ☐	12:15-32 ☐	12:33-42 ☐	12:43—13:2 ☐	13:3-12 ☐
6	13:13-30 ☐	13:31-43 ☐	13:44-58 ☐	14:1-13 ☐	14:14-21 ☐	14:22-36 ☐	15:1-20 ☐
7	15:21-31 ☐	15:32-39 ☐	16:1-12 ☐	16:13-20 ☐	16:21-28 ☐	17:1-13 ☐	17:14-27 ☐
8	18:1-14 ☐	18:15-22 ☐	18:23-35 ☐	19:1-15 ☐	19:16-30 ☐	20:1-16 ☐	20:17-34 ☐
9	21:1-11 ☐	21:12-22 ☐	21:23-32 ☐	21:33-46 ☐	22:1-22 ☐	22:23-33 ☐	22:34-46 ☐
10	23:1-12 ☐	23:13-39 ☐	24:1-14 ☐	24:15-31 ☐	24:32-51 ☐	25:1-13 ☐	25:14-30 ☐
11	25:31-46 ☐	26:1-16 ☐	26:17-35 ☐	26:36-46 ☐	26:47-64 ☐	26:65-75 ☐	27:1-26 ☐
12	27:27-44 ☐	27:45-56 ☐	27:57—28:15 ☐	28:16-20 ☐	Mark 1:1 ☐	1:2-6 ☐	1:7-13 ☐
13	1:14-28 ☐	1:29-45 ☐	2:1-12 ☐	2:13-28 ☐	3:1-19 ☐	3:20-35 ☐	4:1-25 ☐
14	4:26-41 ☐	5:1-20 ☐	5:21-43 ☐	6:1-29 ☐	6:30-56 ☐	7:1-23 ☐	7:24-37 ☐
15	8:1-26 ☐	8:27—9:1 ☐	9:2-29 ☐	9:30-50 ☐	10:1-16 ☐	10:17-34 ☐	10:35-52 ☐
16	11:1-16 ☐	11:17-33 ☐	12:1-27 ☐	12:28-44 ☐	13:1-13 ☐	13:14-37 ☐	14:1-26 ☐
17	14:27-52 ☐	14:53-72 ☐	15:1-15 ☐	15:16-47 ☐	16:1-8 ☐	16:9-20 ☐	Luke 1:1-4 ☐
18	1:5-25 ☐	1:26-46 ☐	1:47-56 ☐	1:57-80 ☐	2:1-8 ☐	2:9-20 ☐	2:21-39 ☐
19	2:40-52 ☐	3:1-20 ☐	3:21-38 ☐	4:1-13 ☐	4:14-30 ☐	4:31-44 ☐	5:1-26 ☐
20	5:27—6:16 ☐	6:17-38 ☐	6:39-49 ☐	7:1-17 ☐	7:18-23 ☐	7:24-35 ☐	7:36-50 ☐
21	8:1-15 ☐	8:16-25 ☐	8:26-39 ☐	8:40-56 ☐	9:1-17 ☐	9:18-26 ☐	9:27-36 ☐
22	9:37-50 ☐	9:51-62 ☐	10:1-11 ☐	10:12-24 ☐	10:25-37 ☐	10:38-42 ☐	11:1-13 ☐
23	11:14-26 ☐	11:27-36 ☐	11:37-54 ☐	12:1-12 ☐	12:13-21 ☐	12:22-34 ☐	12:35-48 ☐
24	12:49-59 ☐	13:1-9 ☐	13:10-17 ☐	13:18-30 ☐	13:31—14:6 ☐	14:7-14 ☐	14:15-24 ☐
25	14:25-35 ☐	15:1-10 ☐	15:11-21 ☐	15:22-32 ☐	16:1-13 ☐	16:14-22 ☐	16:23-31 ☐
26	17:1-19 ☐	17:20-37 ☐	18:1-14 ☐	18:15-30 ☐	18:31-43 ☐	19:1-10 ☐	19:11-27 ☐

Reading Schedule for the Recovery Version of the New Testament with Footnotes

Wk.	Lord's Day	Monday	Tuesday	Wednesday	Thursday	Friday	Saturday
27	Luke 19:28-48 ☐	20:1-19 ☐	20:20-38 ☐	20:39—21:4 ☐	21:5-27 ☐	21:28-38 ☐	22:1-20 ☐
28	22:21-38 ☐	22:39-54 ☐	22:55-71 ☐	23:1-43 ☐	23:44-56 ☐	24:1-12 ☐	24:13-35 ☐
29	24:36-53 ☐	John 1:1-13 ☐	1:14-18 ☐	1:19-34 ☐	1:35-51 ☐	2:1-11 ☐	2:12-22 ☐
30	2:23—3:13 ☐	3:14-21 ☐	3:22-36 ☐	4:1-14 ☐	4:15-26 ☐	4:27-42 ☐	4:43-54 ☐
31	5:1-16 ☐	5:17-30 ☐	5:31-47 ☐	6:1-15 ☐	6:16-31 ☐	6:32-51 ☐	6:52-71 ☐
32	7:1-9 ☐	7:10-24 ☐	7:25-36 ☐	7:37-52 ☐	7:53—8:11 ☐	8:12-27 ☐	8:28-44 ☐
33	8:45-59 ☐	9:1-13 ☐	9:14-34 ☐	9:35—10:9 ☐	10:10-30 ☐	10:31—11:4 ☐	11:5-22 ☐
34	11:23-40 ☐	11:41-57 ☐	12:1-11 ☐	12:12-24 ☐	12:25-36 ☐	12:37-50 ☐	13:1-11 ☐
35	13:12-30 ☐	13:31-38 ☐	14:1-6 ☐	14:7-20 ☐	14:21-31 ☐	15:1-11 ☐	15:12-27 ☐
36	16:1-15 ☐	16:16-33 ☐	17:1-5 ☐	17:6-13 ☐	17:14-24 ☐	17:25—18:11 ☐	18:12-27 ☐
37	18:28-40 ☐	19:1-16 ☐	19:17-30 ☐	19:31-42 ☐	20:1-13 ☐	20:14-18 ☐	20:19-22 ☐
38	20:23-31 ☐	21:1-14 ☐	21:15-22 ☐	21:23-25 ☐	Acts 1:1-8 ☐	1:9-14 ☐	1:15-26 ☐
39	2:1-13 ☐	2:14-21 ☐	2:22-36 ☐	2:37-41 ☐	2:42-47 ☐	3:1-18 ☐	3:19—4:22 ☐
40	4:23-37 ☐	5:1-16 ☐	5:17-32 ☐	5:33-42 ☐	6:1—7:1 ☐	7:2-29 ☐	7:30-60 ☐
41	8:1-13 ☐	8:14-25 ☐	8:26-40 ☐	9:1-19 ☐	9:20-43 ☐	10:1-16 ☐	10:17-33 ☐
42	10:34-48 ☐	11:1-18 ☐	11:19-30 ☐	12:1-25 ☐	13:1-12 ☐	13:13-43 ☐	13:44—14:5 ☐
43	14:6-28 ☐	15:1-12 ☐	15:13-34 ☐	15:35—16:5 ☐	16:6-18 ☐	16:19-40 ☐	17:1-18 ☐
44	17:19-34 ☐	18:1-17 ☐	18:18-28 ☐	19:1-20 ☐	19:21-41 ☐	20:1-12 ☐	20:13-38 ☐
45	21:1-14 ☐	21:15-26 ☐	21:27-40 ☐	22:1-21 ☐	22:22-29 ☐	22:30—23:11 ☐	23:12-15 ☐
46	23:16-30 ☐	23:31—24:21 ☐	24:22—25:5 ☐	25:6-27 ☐	26:1-13 ☐	26:14-32 ☐	27:1-26 ☐
47	27:27—28:10 ☐	28:11-22 ☐	28:23-31 ☐	Rom. 1:1-2 ☐	1:3-7 ☐	1:8-17 ☐	1:18-25 ☐
48	1:26—2:10 ☐	2:11-29 ☐	3:1-20 ☐	3:21-31 ☐	4:1-12 ☐	4:13-25 ☐	5:1-11 ☐
49	5:12-17 ☐	5:18—6:5 ☐	6:6-11 ☐	6:12-23 ☐	7:1-12 ☐	7:13-25 ☐	8:1-2 ☐
50	8:3-6 ☐	8:7-13 ☐	8:14-25 ☐	8:26-39 ☐	9:1-18 ☐	9:19—10:3 ☐	10:4-15 ☐
51	10:16—11:10 ☐	11:11-22 ☐	11:23-36 ☐	12:1-3 ☐	12:4-21 ☐	13:1-14 ☐	14:1-12 ☐
52	14:13-23 ☐	15:1-13 ☐	15:14-33 ☐	16:1-5 ☐	16:6-24 ☐	16:25-27 ☐	1 Cor. 1:1-4 ☐

Reading Schedule for the Recovery Version of the New Testament with Footnotes

Wk.	Lord's Day	Monday	Tuesday	Wednesday	Thursday	Friday	Saturday
53	1 Cor. 1:5-9 ☐	1:10-17 ☐	1:18-31 ☐	2:1-5 ☐	2:6-10 ☐	2:11-16 ☐	3:1-9 ☐
54	3:10-13 ☐	3:14-23 ☐	4:1-9 ☐	4:10-21 ☐	5:1-13 ☐	6:1-11 ☐	6:12-20 ☐
55	7:1-16 ☐	7:17-24 ☐	7:25-40 ☐	8:1-13 ☐	9:1-15 ☐	9:16-27 ☐	10:1-4 ☐
56	10:5-13 ☐	10:14-33 ☐	11:1-6 ☐	11:7-16 ☐	11:17-26 ☐	11:27-34 ☐	12:1-11 ☐
57	12:12-22 ☐	12:23-31 ☐	13:1-13 ☐	14:1-12 ☐	14:13-25 ☐	14:26-33 ☐	14:34-40 ☐
58	15:1-19 ☐	15:20-28 ☐	15:29-34 ☐	15:35-49 ☐	15:50-58 ☐	16:1-9 ☐	16:10-24 ☐
59	2 Cor. 1:1-4 ☐	1:5-14 ☐	1:15-22 ☐	1:23—2:11 ☐	2:12-17 ☐	3:1-6 ☐	3:7-11 ☐
60	3:12-18 ☐	4:1-6 ☐	4:7-12 ☐	4:13-18 ☐	5:1-8 ☐	5:9-15 ☐	5:16-21 ☐
61	6:1-13 ☐	6:14—7:4 ☐	7:5-16 ☐	8:1-15 ☐	8:16-24 ☐	9:1-15 ☐	10:1-6 ☐
62	10:7-18 ☐	11:1-15 ☐	11:16-33 ☐	12:1-10 ☐	12:11-21 ☐	13:1-10 ☐	13:11-14 ☐
63	Gal. 1:1-5 ☐	1:6-14 ☐	1:15-24 ☐	2:1-13 ☐	2:14-21 ☐	3:1-4 ☐	3:5-14 ☐
64	3:15-22 ☐	3:23-29 ☐	4:1-7 ☐	4:8-20 ☐	4:21-31 ☐	5:1-12 ☐	5:13-21 ☐
65	5:22-26 ☐	6:1-10 ☐	6:11-15 ☐	6:16-18 ☐	Eph. 1:1-3 ☐	1:4-6 ☐	1:7-10 ☐
66	1:11-14 ☐	1:15-18 ☐	1:19-23 ☐	2:1-5 ☐	2:6-10 ☐	2:11-14 ☐	2:15-18 ☐
67	2:19-22 ☐	3:1-7 ☐	3:8-13 ☐	3:14-18 ☐	3:19-21 ☐	4:1-4 ☐	4:5-10 ☐
68	4:11-16 ☐	4:17-24 ☐	4:25-32 ☐	5:1-10 ☐	5:11-21 ☐	5:22-26 ☐	5:27-33 ☐
69	6:1-9 ☐	6:10-14 ☐	6:15-18 ☐	6:19-24 ☐	Phil. 1:1-7 ☐	1:8-18 ☐	1:19-26 ☐
70	1:27—2:4 ☐	2:5-11 ☐	2:12-16 ☐	2:17-30 ☐	3:1-6 ☐	3:7-11 ☐	3:12-16 ☐
71	3:17-21 ☐	4:1-9 ☐	4:10-23 ☐	Col. 1:1-8 ☐	1:9-13 ☐	1:14-23 ☐	1:24-29 ☐
72	2:1-7 ☐	2:8-15 ☐	2:16-23 ☐	3:1-4 ☐	3:5-15 ☐	3:16-25 ☐	4:1-18 ☐
73	1 Thes. 1:1-3 ☐	1:4-10 ☐	2:1-12 ☐	2:13—3:5 ☐	3:6-13 ☐	4:1-10 ☐	4:11—5:11 ☐
74	5:12-28 ☐	2 Thes. 1:1-12 ☐	2:1-17 ☐	3:1-18 ☐	1 Tim. 1:1-2 ☐	1:3-4 ☐	1:5-14 ☐
75	1:15-20 ☐	2:1-7 ☐	2:8-15 ☐	3:1-13 ☐	3:14—4:5 ☐	4:6-16 ☐	5:1-25 ☐
76	6:1-10 ☐	6:11-21 ☐	2 Tim. 1:1-10 ☐	1:11-18 ☐	2:1-15 ☐	2:16-26 ☐	3:1-13 ☐
77	3:14—4:8 ☐	4:9-22 ☐	Titus 1:1-4 ☐	1:5-16 ☐	2:1-15 ☐	3:1-8 ☐	3:9-15 ☐
78	Philem. 1:1-11 ☐	1:12-25 ☐	Heb. 1:1-2 ☐	1:3-5 ☐	1:6-14 ☐	2:1-9 ☐	2:10-18 ☐

Reading Schedule for the Recovery Version of the New Testament with Footnotes

Wk.	Lord's Day	Monday	Tuesday	Wednesday	Thursday	Friday	Saturday
79	Heb. 3:1-6 ☐	3:7-19 ☐	4:1-9 ☐	4:10-13 ☐	4:14-16 ☐	5:1-10 ☐	5:11—6:3 ☐
80	6:4-8 ☐	6:9-20 ☐	7:1-10 ☐	7:11-28 ☐	8:1-6 ☐	8:7-13 ☐	9:1-4 ☐
81	9:5-14 ☐	9:15-28 ☐	10:1-18 ☐	10:19-28 ☐	10:29-39 ☐	11:1-6 ☐	11:7-19 ☐
82	11:20-31 ☐	11:32-40 ☐	12:1-2 ☐	12:3-13 ☐	12:14-17 ☐	12:18-26 ☐	12:27-29 ☐
83	13:1-7 ☐	13:8-12 ☐	13:13-15 ☐	13:16-25 ☐	James 1:1-8 ☐	1:9-18 ☐	1:19-27 ☐
84	2:1-13 ☐	2:14-26 ☐	3:1-18 ☐	4:1-10 ☐	4:11-17 ☐	5:1-12 ☐	5:13-20 ☐
85	1 Pet. 1:1-2 ☐	1:3-4 ☐	1:5 ☐	1:6-9 ☐	1:10-12 ☐	1:13-17 ☐	1:18-25 ☐
86	2:1-3 ☐	2:4-8 ☐	2:9-17 ☐	2:18-25 ☐	3:1-13 ☐	3:14-22 ☐	4:1-6 ☐
87	4:7-16 ☐	4:17-19 ☐	5:1-4 ☐	5:5-9 ☐	5:10-14 ☐	2 Pet. 1:1-2 ☐	1:3-4 ☐
88	1:5-8 ☐	1:9-11 ☐	1:12-18 ☐	1:19-21 ☐	2:1-3 ☐	2:4-11 ☐	2:12-22 ☐
89	3:1-6 ☐	3:7-9 ☐	3:10-12 ☐	3:13-15 ☐	3:16 ☐	3:17-18 ☐	1 John 1:1-2 ☐
90	1:3-4 ☐	1:5 ☐	1:6 ☐	1:7 ☐	1:8-10 ☐	2:1-2 ☐	2:3-11 ☐
91	2:12-14 ☐	2:15-19 ☐	2:20-23 ☐	2:24-27 ☐	2:28-29 ☐	3:1-5 ☐	3:6-10 ☐
92	3:11-18 ☐	3:19-24 ☐	4:1-6 ☐	4:7-11 ☐	4:12-15 ☐	4:16—5:3 ☐	5:4-13 ☐
93	5:14-17 ☐	5:18-21 ☐	2 John 1:1-3 ☐	1:4-9 ☐	1:10-13 ☐	3 John 1:1-6 ☐	1:7-14 ☐
94	Jude 1:1-4 ☐	1:5-10 ☐	1:11-19 ☐	1:20-25 ☐	Rev. 1:1-3 ☐	1:4-6 ☐	1:7-11 ☐
95	1:12-13 ☐	1:14-16 ☐	1:17-20 ☐	2:1-6 ☐	2:7 ☐	2:8-9 ☐	2:10-11 ☐
96	2:12-14 ☐	2:15-17 ☐	2:18-23 ☐	2:24-29 ☐	3:1-3 ☐	3:4-6 ☐	3:7-9 ☐
97	3:10-13 ☐	3:14-18 ☐	3:19-22 ☐	4:1-5 ☐	4:6-7 ☐	4:8-11 ☐	5:1-6 ☐
98	5:7-14 ☐	6:1-8 ☐	6:9-17 ☐	7:1-8 ☐	7:9-17 ☐	8:1-6 ☐	8:7-12 ☐
99	8:13—9:11 ☐	9:12-21 ☐	10:1-4 ☐	10:5-11 ☐	11:1-4 ☐	11:5-14 ☐	11:15-19 ☐
100	12:1-4 ☐	12:5-9 ☐	12:10-18 ☐	13:1-10 ☐	13:11-18 ☐	14:1-5 ☐	14:6-12 ☐
101	14:13-20 ☐	15:1-8 ☐	16:1-12 ☐	16:13-21 ☐	17:1-6 ☐	17:7-18 ☐	18:1-8 ☐
102	18:9—19:4 ☐	19:5-10 ☐	19:11-16 ☐	19:17-21 ☐	20:1-6 ☐	20:7-10 ☐	20:11-15 ☐
103	21:1 ☐	21:2 ☐	21:3-8 ☐	21:9-13 ☐	21:14-18 ☐	21:19-21 ☐	21:22-27 ☐
104	22:1 ☐	22:2 ☐	22:3-11 ☐	22:12-15 ☐	22:16-17 ☐	22:18-21 ☐	

Week 13 — Day 4	Today's verses	Week 13 — Day 5	Today's verses	Week 13 — Day 6	Today's verses

Week 13 — Day 4   Today's verses

Heb. Now no discipline at the present time
12:11 seems to be *a matter* of joy, but of grief; but afterward it yields the peaceable fruit of righteousness to those who have been exercised by it.

Rom. And we know that all things work to-
8:28 gether for good to those who love God, to those who are called according to *His* purpose.

_____
Date

Week 13 — Day 5   Today's verses

Gal. For neither is circumcision anything nor
6:15-16 uncircumcision, but a new creation *is what matters*. And as many as walk by this rule, peace be upon them and mercy, even upon the Israel of God.

_____
Date

Week 13 — Day 6   Today's verses

1 Thes. Paul and Silvanus and Timothy to the
1:1 church of the Thessalonians in God the Father and the Lord Jesus Christ: Grace to you and peace.

Matt. Go therefore and disciple all the nations,
28:19 baptizing them into the name of the Father and of the Son and of the Holy Spirit.

_____
Date

Week 13 — Day 1   Today's verses

Exo. ...Thus you shall say to the children of Is-
3:15-16 rael, Jehovah, the God of your fathers, the God of Abraham, the God of Isaac, and the God of Jacob, has sent me to you. This is My name forever, and this is My memorial from generation to generation. Go, and gather the elders of Israel together, and say to them, Jehovah, the God of your fathers, the God of Abraham, of Isaac, and of Jacob, has appeared to me...

_____
Date

Week 13 — Day 2   Today's verses

Rom. (As it is written, "I have appointed you a
4:17 father of many nations") in the sight of God whom he believed, who gives life to the dead and calls the things not being as being.

11:36 Because out from Him and through Him and to Him are all things. To Him be the glory forever. Amen.

_____
Date

Week 13 — Day 3   Today's verses

Gen. And Sarah my master's wife bore a son to
24:36 my master after she had become old. And he has given all that he has to him.

1 Cor. For who distinguishes you? And what do
4:7 you have that you did not receive? And if you did receive *it*, why do you boast as though not having received *it*?

_____
Date

Week 14 — Day 4 — Today's verses

Gen. And Jehovah appeared to Abram and said,
12:7 To your seed I will give this land. And
there he built an altar to Jehovah who had
appeared to him.

13:3-4 And he continued on his journey from the
Negev as far as Bethel, to the place where
his tent had been at the beginning, between Bethel and Ai, to the place of the
altar, which he had made there formerly;
and there Abram called on the name of
Jehovah.

_____
Date

Week 14 — Day 5 — Today's verses

Gen. And Abram passed through the land to the
12:6-8 place of Shechem, to the oak of Moreh....
And Jehovah appeared to Abram....And
there he built an altar to Jehovah who had
appeared to him. And he...pitched his
tent, with Bethel on the west and Ai on the
east; and there he built an altar to Jehovah
and called upon the name of Jehovah.

_____
Date

Week 14 — Day 6 — Today's verses

Gen. And Abram moved his tent and came and
13:18 dwelt by the oaks of Mamre, which are in
Hebron, and there he built an altar to
Jehovah.

Rev. And I saw the holy city, New Jerusalem,
21:2-3 coming down out of heaven from God....
Behold, the tabernacle of God is with
men, and He will tabernacle with them...

_____
Date

Week 14 — Day 1 — Today's verses

Rom. And the father of circumcision to those...
4:12 who also walk in the steps of that faith of
our father Abraham, which *he had* in
uncircumcision.

Gal. Know then that they who are of faith,
3:7 these are sons of Abraham.

14 In order that the blessing of Abraham
might come to the Gentiles in Christ Jesus, that we might receive the promise of
the Spirit through faith.

_____
Date

Week 14 — Day 2 — Today's verses

Heb. Let us therefore come forward with bold-
4:16 ness to the throne of grace that we may
receive mercy and find grace for timely
help.

13:13 Let us therefore go forth unto Him outside
the camp, bearing His reproach.

6:1 ...Let us be brought on to maturity, not
laying again a foundation of repentance
from dead works and of faith in God.

_____
Date

Week 14 — Day 3 — Today's verses

Acts ...The God of glory appeared to our father
7:2 Abraham while he was in Mesopotamia...

John Jesus said to them, Truly, truly, I say to you,
8:58 Before Abraham came into being, I am.

Heb. By faith Abraham, being called, obeyed to
11:8 go out unto a place which he was to receive as an inheritance; and he went out,
not knowing where he was going.

_____
Date

Week 15 — Day 4   Today's verses

Gen. But then the word of Jehovah came to him,
15:4-5 saying, This man shall not be your heir, but he who will come out from your own body shall be your heir. And He brought him outside and said, Look now toward the heavens, and count the stars, if you are able to count them. And He said to him, So shall your seed be.

_____
Date

Week 15 — Day 5   Today's verses

Gen. And he believed Jehovah, and He ac-
15:6 counted it to him as righteousness.

Rom. For if Abraham was justified out of works,
4:2-3 he has something to boast in, but not before God. For what does the Scripture say? "And Abraham believed God, and it was accounted to him as righteousness."

_____
Date

Week 15 — Day 6   Today's verses

Rom. For it was not through the law that the
4:13 promise was made to Abraham or to his seed that he would be the heir of the world, but through the righteousness of faith.

12:5 So we who are many are one Body in Christ, and individually members one of another.

_____
Date

Week 15 — Day 1   Today's verses

Gen. And Jehovah appeared to Abram and said,
12:7 To your seed I will give this land...

Gal. But to Abraham were the promises spo-
3:16 ken and to his seed. He does not say, And to the seeds, as concerning many, but as concerning one: "And to your seed," who is Christ.

_____
Date

Week 15 — Day 2   Today's verses

Gal. Christ has redeemed us out of the curse of
3:13-14 the law, having become a curse on our behalf; because it is written, "Cursed is everyone hanging on a tree"; in order that the blessing of Abraham might come to the Gentiles in Christ Jesus, that we might receive the promise of the Spirit through faith.

_____
Date

Week 15 — Day 3   Today's verses

Gal. Know then that they who are of faith,
3:7 these are sons of Abraham.

26 For you are all sons of God through faith in Christ Jesus.

29 And if you are of Christ, then you are Abraham's seed, heirs according to promise.

_____
Date

Week 16 — Day 4   Today's verses

1 Cor. For even as the body is one and has many
12:12-13 members, yet all the members of the body, being many, are one body, so also is the Christ. For also in one Spirit we were all baptized into one Body, whether Jews or Greeks, whether slaves or free, and were all given to drink one Spirit.

Eph. In whom you also are being built together
2:22 into a dwelling place of God in spirit.

Date

Week 16 — Day 5   Today's verses

Gen. And He said to him, Bring Me a three-
15:9 year-old heifer and a three-year-old female goat and a three-year-old ram and a turtledove and a young pigeon.

John Jesus said..., I am the resurrection and the
11:25 life; he who believes into Me, even if he should die, shall live.

14:19 Yet a little while and the world beholds Me no longer, but you behold Me; because I live, you also shall live.

Date

Week 16 — Day 6   Today's verses

Rom. Now if we have died with Christ, we be-
6:8 lieve that we will also live with Him.

Gal. I am crucified with Christ; and *it is* no longer I
2:20 *who* live, but *it is* Christ *who* lives in me; and the *life* which I now live in the flesh I live in faith, the *faith* of the Son of God, who loved me and gave Himself up for me.

Date

Week 16 — Day 1   Today's verses

Gen. And Jehovah appeared to Abram and said,
12:7 To your seed I will give this land...

13:14-15 And Jehovah said to Abram after Lot had separated from him, Now lift up your eyes, and look from the place where you are, northward and southward and eastward and westward; for all the land that you see I will give to you and to your seed forever.

Date

Week 16 — Day 2   Today's verses

Col. Giving thanks to the Father, who has qual-
1:12 ified you for a share of the allotted portion of the saints in the light.

2:6 As therefore you have received the Christ, Jesus the Lord, walk in Him.

Gal. But I say, Walk by the Spirit and you shall
5:16 by no means fulfill the lust of the flesh.

Date

Week 16 — Day 3   Today's verses

Gal. In order that the blessing of Abraham
3:14 might come to the Gentiles in Christ Jesus, that we might receive the promise of the Spirit through faith.

1 Cor. ...The last Adam *became* a life-giving
15:45 Spirit.

Date

Week 17 — Day 4 — Today's verses

Heb. If indeed then perfection were through
7:11 the Levitical priesthood…, what need was there still that a different Priest should arise according to the order of Melchizedek and that He should not be said to be according to the order of Aaron?

25 Hence also He is able to save to the uttermost those who come forward to God through Him, since He lives always to intercede for them.

Date

Week 17 — Day 5 — Today's verses

Psa. Your people will offer themselves will-
110:3-4 ingly in the day of Your warfare, in the splendor of their consecration. Your young men will be to You like the dew from the womb of the dawn. Jehovah has sworn, and He will not change: You are a Priest forever according to the order of Melchizedek.

Date

Week 17 — Day 6 — Today's verses

Gen. But Abram said to the king of Sodom, I
14:22-23 have lifted up my hand to Jehovah, God the Most High, Possessor of heaven and earth, that I will not take a thread or a sandal thong, or anything that is yours, lest you say, I have made Abram rich.

Date

Week 17 — Day 1 — Today's verses

Gen. So Lot chose for himself the entire plain of
13:11-12 the Jordan, and Lot journeyed east; and they separated themselves from each other. Abram dwelt in the land of Canaan, and Lot dwelt in the cities of the plain and moved his tent as far as Sodom.

Date

Week 17 — Day 2 — Today's verses

Gen. And when Abram heard that his brother
14:14-16 had been taken captive, he led out his trained men, born in his house, three hundred eighteen of them, and pursued as far as Dan. And he… struck them….And he brought back all the possessions and also brought back Lot his brother and his possessions as well as the women and the people.

Date

Week 17 — Day 3 — Today's verses

Gen. And Melchizedek the king of Salem brought
14:18-20 out bread and wine. Now he was priest of God the Most High. And he blessed him and said, Blessed be Abram of God the Most High, Possessor of heaven and earth; and blessed be God the Most High, who has delivered your enemies into your hand…

Date

Week 18 — Day 4   Today's verses

Col. In Him also you were circumcised with a
2:11 circumcision not made with hands, in the
putting off of the body of the flesh, in the
circumcision of Christ.

Phil. For we are the circumcision, the ones
3:3 who serve by the Spirit of God and boast
in Christ Jesus and have no confidence in
the flesh.

_____
Date

Week 18 — Day 5   Today's verses

Gal. And the Scripture, foreseeing that God
3:8 would justify the Gentiles out of faith, announced the gospel beforehand to Abraham: "In you shall all the nations be
blessed."

26 For you are all sons of God through faith
in Christ Jesus.

_____
Date

Week 18 — Day 6   Today's verses

Gal. But the Jerusalem above is free, which is our
4:26 mother.

Heb. But you have come forward to Mount Zion
12:22-23 and to the city of the living God, the heavenly Jerusalem…and to the church of the
firstborn…

_____
Date

Week 18 — Day 1   Today's verses

Gal. For it is written that Abraham had two
4:22-24 sons, one of the maidservant and one of
the free woman. However the one of the
maidservant was born according to the
flesh, but the one of the free woman *was
born* through promise. These things are
spoken allegorically, for these women are
two covenants…

_____
Date

Week 18 — Day 2   Today's verses

Gal. Now this Hagar is Sinai the mountain in
4:25 Arabia and corresponds to the Jerusalem
which now is, for she is in slavery with her
children.

5:1 *It is* for freedom *that* Christ has set us free;
stand fast therefore, and do not be entangled with a yoke of slavery again.

_____
Date

Week 18 — Day 3   Today's verses

Gal. You have been brought to nought, *sepa-
5:4 rated* from Christ, you who are being justified by law; you have fallen from grace.

4:30 …"Cast out the maidservant and her son,
for the son of the maidservant shall by no
means inherit with the son of the free
woman."

_____
Date